Running to the Fire

sightline books

The Iowa Series in Literary Nonfiction

Patricia Hampl & Carl H. Klaus, series editors

Tim Bascom
Running to the Fire

An American Missionary Comes of Age in Revolutionary Ethiopia

University of Iowa Press   Iowa City

University of Iowa Press, Iowa City 52242
Copyright © 2015 by the University of Iowa Press
www.uiowapress.org
Printed in the United States of America
Text design by Richard Hendel

The University of Iowa Press is a member of
Green Press Initiative and is committed to
preserving natural resources.

Printed on acid-free paper

ISBN: 978-1-60938-328-2 (pbk)
ISBN: 978-1-60938-329-9 (ebk)

Library of Congress Cataloging-in-Publication Data is
on file at the Library of Congress

This book is dedicated to all those who have been forced by war to leave their homes, starting over in foreign lands, particularly the hundreds of thousands of refugees from northeast Africa, people who have been driven out of Ethiopia, Eritrea, Somalia, and Sudan.

Contents

Acknowledgments

Memoir is an imperfect attempt to recreate historical events. It is shaded by the author's perceptions. It is distorted by the act of organizing. However, here is my attempt to be true to what I remember. Occasionally I have collapsed time or changed a name. Here and there, I have borrowed facts from research rather than direct observation. Nevertheless, the events in this story are, to the best of my knowledge, real events from real history.

Much appreciation to those fellow writers who have helped me develop this account: Andy Douglas, Amy Kolen, Cecile Goding, Lois Cole, Eric Jones, Carol Roh-Spaulding, Karen Bradway, Josh Doležal, Kay Bascom, and Daniel Coleman. Thanks to the writers listed at the end of the book, too, whose published books were an invaluable resource, and to my insightful editors, Carl Klaus and Elisabeth Chretien. In addition, thanks to the Collegeville Institute at St. John's University in Minnesota for giving me time to write. And thanks to Drake University Center for the Humanities, the Iowa Arts Council, and the National Endowment for the Humanities for funding a research trip to Ethiopia.

Special gratitude goes out to several other encouragers: Patricia Foster, Sigrid Till, and Jo Wetherell. Also, to my creative sons Luke and Connor, who have listened with interest. And to my wife Cathleen, who has given me great advice over the years, believing in my writing even when I lost faith. And, finally, I thank my parents and brothers for letting me tell my version of what happened.

Let me note that two portions of the memoir were published in earlier forms: "Checkpoint" (Runner-up for The Florida Review Editors' Prize, 2011) and "Bicentennial Pie" (selected for the anthology *Fried Walleye and Cherry Pie*, edited by Peggy Wolff, University of Nebraska Press, 2013).

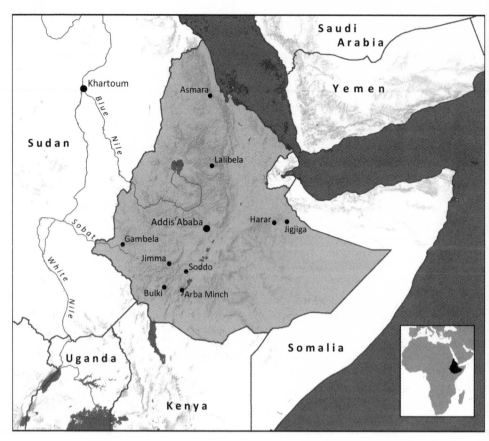

Map of Ethiopia in 1977.
Designed by Audrey Hughey and Dr. Johnathan Bascom.

Here is how Ethiopia appeared in 1977 at the height of the Marxist revolution led by Colonel Mengistu and his shadowy Derg (Committee of Equals). While waging an internal war against counter-revolutionaries, the Derg battled a rebel army from the north, which eventually won independence for Eritrea (capital of Asmara, 1993). The Derg also fought a war with Somalia, which began to invade the Ogaden Desert in 1977, putting the city of Jigjiga under siege.

Whereas today the eastern portion of Ethiopia is predominately Muslim, the area north of the capital, Addis Ababa, remains a stronghold of the Orthodox church (including Lalibela, where twelve monolithic carved churches stand from the twelfth-century reign of King Lalibela). In the early twentieth century, as Emperor Selassie allowed Western mission agencies to enter the country, he decreed that they could not evangelize in the Orthodox north, concentrating instead on animist regions of the south—thus the cluster of mission stations at cities such as Jimma, Soddo, Arba Minch, and Bulki.

Finally, note the Nile and Sobat rivers in Sudan, which served as an early entry route for missionaries coming to Ethiopia. The famous missionary-explorer Dr. David Livingstone predicted in the 1860s that the Nile would bring Westerners into the region and help to end the East African slave trade, which proved to be true.

Lit

A city set on a hill cannot be hidden. Neither do people light a lamp
and put it under a bowl. Instead they put it on a stand and it gives
light to everyone in the house.

MATTHEW 5.14

. . . revolution is necessary, therefore, not only because the ruling
class cannot be overthrown in any other way, but also because the
class overthrowing it can only in a revolution succeed in ridding
itself of all the muck of ages and become fitted to found
society anew.

KARL MARX

One

The bus is swaying along seven thousand feet above sea level, covered with fine red dust, when we come upon an incredibly deep ravine and a narrow bridge and two sentries lounging behind a half-circle of sandbags with a mounted machine gun perched next to them like a praying mantis. The brakes squeal. The sentries straighten. And the old man who has fallen asleep against me starts to fall forward before catching himself and lifting his woolly head, smelling of woodsmoke.

"Awzunalow," he says, apologizing as he pats my leg.

While blood rushes back into my numb shoulder, I look to my father and see that his jaw muscles are popping. He lifts a hand to knead his forehead where the receding hairline has created a black prong of hair. He grimaces at me in a sympathetic way.

I have grown accustomed to checkpoints in Addis Ababa, where many of the neighborhood police recognize the bus from my boarding school. But here, 124 miles to the south, I know, as he does, that nothing will be predictable, especially since the two of us are probably the only foreigners these sentries have seen for a month. Westerners with Western clothes and haircuts. From America, no less. Enemies of the state. And the younger one—that's me—acting like one of the Beatles, with a mop of black hair and a smile turned up at one corner as if hiding ironic thoughts.

The soldiers step onto the bus, unslinging their Kalashnikov weapons. They order everyone off, and as we file forward, I spot an officer emerging from his sentry shack. He is thin and haughty with latte-colored skin and a mouth pinned down by slit-like wrinkles. He stretches as if easing an ache. At his back are the shrouded peaks of several mountains. Down the rocky scree, beside a torrent of yellow water, lies another bus like ours, only it is flipped on its side like a discarded toy.

I feel the old wariness of being back in the "battle zone." For three weeks I have relaxed my guard while ensconced in a remote mountain pass where my parents are trying to revive an abandoned medical clinic. Out there, I have allowed myself to act as if the Ethiopian revolution is someone else's bad dream. Now, however, the sullen sentries and the wary travelers bring it home: the war is not over yet.

I assume these guards will demand that a few passengers open their bags, starting with us. I am right, which means everyone stands around curiously as the driver sends his servant boy up to untie our suitcases and toss them down. The burgundy Samsonites stand out next to all the cloth bundles and wooden crates. What might lie inside? The crowd cranes while the soldiers unclasp my case and then my father's. Everyone is curious except the old man who slept on my shoulder. Instead, he clucks, shaking his peppery head. When I glance at him, he shrugs as if to say, "What can you do?"

I am glad the guards seem bored, rummaging through the folded clothing. Then one of them bumps Dad's Bible into the open and their officer steps forward.

"Why do you write here?" he asks in English, flipping through the marked pages.

"It's a way to remember things."

"Why do you need to remember?"

I can feel my face tighten. I will have no control over how my father responds, and I know he will feel obligated, as always, to share what he believes.

"The Bible is like a map from God," Dad says. "It tells us how to live."

"No," says the soldier, sneering. "Don't you know, this book keeps people sleeping. This stops us becoming strong."

Dad smiles a little too warmly. "Why would God want to make us weak?" he asks.

The soldier curls his lip. He glares. "What are you? Missionary?"

I taste hot citrus at the back of my throat, remembering the water I boiled from our cistern just yesterday and how I tried to mask its rancid flavor with powdered Tang, forcing myself not to think of the dead rat I found floating in the tank. I want to reach across and cover my father's mouth. I want him to shake his head and get back onto the bus. Let them have the Bible. We can get another.

But he doesn't hesitate. "Yes, I am a missionary. A doctor, too."

"You are doctor, but you think Bible is good?"

"Yes."

As the officer sneers, contemplating his options, I feel the primal tension of being a son—proud of my father's courage yet embarrassed, longing to emulate him yet troubled, not sure (to be brutally honest) whether I trust his vision of the world and of a God who presumably hovers over it all, always safely in command. Is God really there taking note, ready to intervene if necessary?

Maybe, I think, we shouldn't have come back to Ethiopia. Maybe we should have just stayed in Kansas.

Two

hen I first wrote this book, I didn't break in like I'm doing right here—you know, talking directly to you. It was an entertaining story about some other guy I used to be back in a more dramatic era—a kind of nonfiction novel of the action/adventure sort.

However, true memoirs provide not just a younger version of the self; they provide an older self looking back and trying to make sense of what happened. So here I am in duplex—a kind of double whammy. Two for the price of one.

The older version of myself can tell you stuff that the boy never knew or tried to comprehend. He can unroll the scroll of his retrospective thoughts, tracing speculations he's not sure he should admit, since they could threaten his well-rehearsed family version of the past. Take, for instance, the realization that his mother had already begun to learn self-denial long before her dramatic college-age conversion, having been forced to surrender her goals starting in junior high, when her frail mother had a nervous breakdown and disappeared into the bedroom. Or take his speculation about his father, who made a perfect match for this selfless spouse, having struggled all through his youth with ego-absorbed depression and having felt set loose only when he devoted himself to the radical Jesus of the Bible.

"Come, and I will make you fishers of men." That's what my dad heard partway through his medical school years—and Mom too, who had just had a realization that she amounted to nothing really, and that it didn't matter because God still loved her.

"Put down your nets and your old dreams. Leave behind your parents, your siblings too. Don't look back. Just come."

So they did—the two of them yoked together as a wholly committed team. And they kept doing it with my brothers and me in tow, taking us overseas first for five years in the 1960s, and then again in 1977, right in the middle of a Marxist revolution.

Between these missionary stints, however, there was a little town in Kansas not far from where my frail, heart-palpitating grandmother lived. And that is where I stayed long enough to almost completely put away what I recalled of Ethiopia—remaining through fourth grade and right up to my sophomore year in high school. Troy was the name of the sheltering town, nestled in a big bow of the Missouri River, and it was there I started my lifelong attempt to belong in the United States, learning for a while how to be a proper Kansan, a red-blooded Midwestern teen. Getting so good at it, in fact, that when a pivotal date came and went—September 12, 1974—I had no idea that it had changed everything, no idea that my family's future had just begun to realign in ways I could not foresee or stop.

Three

he first reports arrived in the *St. Joseph Gazette*, tossed in our driveway: "Emperor Dethroned."

It wasn't major news, not for most of our neighbors, who were fixed on larger headlines that had to do with the fall of an even bigger "emperor"—President Nixon, who had resigned only a month before to avoid impeachment. Next to such grand American scandal, what was the demise of an eighty-year-old ruler who had lost his grip on a small, impoverished country?

In our house, though, Hailie Selassie's overthrow got close attention. My parents shook their heads as they read about a group of military leaders—the Committee of Equals—declaring Ethiopia a socialist state, then forcing the emperor, ruler for over four decades, to exit his palace in a Volkswagen Bug. They sighed as they read snippets to my brothers and me. They were stunned because, even though we no longer talked about it much, we had lived in Ethiopia before coming to Troy. We had even met the emperor when he came to our region and toured the mission hospital.

I was intrigued, naturally, and I felt bad about what was happening to Hailie Selassie, whom I admired in an abstract way. But I didn't share my parents' full distress. After all, I was thirteen and not in Ethiopia anymore, which meant it seemed a long way away, eclipsed by life in America. Having a wide-eyed love of the present and having adjusted to this new realm as a grade-school and junior-high kid, I was more Kansan now than anything else, and more interested in looming teenage concerns than far-removed politics. In fact, that summer—the summer before eighth grade—I had hardly even noticed our own president's demise, which played like a whispered backdrop behind the loud, physical action of my adolescent life.

I had spent most afternoons at the town pool, where I kept myself entertained by dunking or getting dunked. As I ran up and down the hot cement, slowing only if the lifeguard whistled, I wasn't worried about the Watergate scandal. I wasn't paying attention to the Vietnam-era draft dodgers coming home from Canada or the expanding tensions of the Cold War in places like Nicaragua or my former haunt, Ethiopia. I was more concerned about doing flips off the diving board without smacking my back or avoiding the guys who were sneaking up on people underwater, then trying to pull their swim trunks down.

I sang along with Eric Clapton on the PA system—"I Shot the Sheriff"—only vaguely aware that something big was unfolding in Washington, D.C. I probably wouldn't have noticed at all except that the radio DJs kept making outraged comments about Nixon's involvement in some sort of hotel break-in, mocking his attempt to pay hush money: "You could get a million dollars . . . I know where it could be gotten. It is not easy, but it could be done."

What did such problems have to do with me, I thought? I couldn't vote. Besides, as a Christian, wasn't I supposed to regard all politics as suspect? Render unto Caesar what is Caesar's—but keep your trust in God. That's what the Sunday school teachers taught us down at First Baptist Church on Main Street.

My parents, in keeping with that mindset, maintained a careful political neutrality, concerned with the kingdom of heaven more than earth. Except, that is, if the politics were clearly opposed to their views—or clearly aligned, as was the case when it came to Emperor Hailie Selassie. Back in the 1930s and 1940s, Selassie had opened the door for Western missions, granting land for hospitals and schools. As a result, he had become a well-regarded figure among missionaries, all the more so because he was a king in the grand, old biblical sense. After all, what other modern-day ruler could rightfully claim to be a descendant of King Solomon and the Queen of Sheba, going by the ancient Hebrew title "The Lion of Judah"?

So when my father reread the account of the coup d'état from the *St. Joseph Gazette*, my mother sighed heavily, and my older brother Johnathan, who was a rather studious high school student, lowered his brows in a frown. By contrast, my younger brother Nat and I dug back into our mashed potatoes and peas, too eager about watching *Happy Days* to get all bent out of shape.

It would take another decade or two for me to appreciate why my parents and older brother were so stunned that afternoon. Hailie Selassie, as I realized over time, carried a huge reputation for such a small man, only five feet four inches tall. After all, his personal destiny had been linked inextricably with the destiny of the entire nation. He had survived exile during the Italian occupation of World War II. He had given Ethiopia a constitution, abolished slavery, built a university, secured one of the first airlines in Africa, led the way toward the founding of the Organization of African Unity. Whole generations of schoolchildren had seen his portrait hung by decree, higher than any other decoration in the classroom, memorizing the hawk-like nose right along with their alphabet—admiring the sharp-brimmed pilot's cap and the medals on his chest as they practiced their subtraction.

To destroy such a revered leader, the rebels had to create an alternate picture. Even before they rushed Selassie to secret house arrest, they began exposing his bourgeoisie excesses on the only Ethiopian TV station, getting the word out through the latest technology, not unlike what the Egyptian protesters would do in Tahrir Square forty years later with their cell phones and Twitter. First, the rebels showed footage of the emperor at a sumptuous banquet table with gilded platters of food, dropping scraps to his Chihuahua. Then they cut to scenes from a recent famine, a terrible catastrophe that the aged ruler had refused to acknowledge. Bony, bloated toddlers appeared on the screen, sitting in the dust. Then the Chihuahua with his chunk of meat. Then the toddlers with flies all over their faces.

I knew none of this back then. And had I been told, I probably would have recoiled in disbelief. I would have echoed my parents as they protested that it was just "communist propaganda." In fact, even as an adult, after learning about those infamous video clips, it would take me years to accept that Selassie really had been so callous, refusing to listen to the pleas of fifteen hundred emaciated farmers who trekked down from the northern highlands to deliver their awful news: "We are dying. All of us are dying."

A year passed, and my parents' attention kept turning more toward Ethiopia, renewed in a strangely insistent way. As we shifted into the summer of 1975, I steeled myself for high school by working in the hayfields, getting thinner and tougher from swinging bales onto a flatbed trailer. I started feeling more aggressive in a new, unfamiliar way—more restless and opinionated. More interested in girls as well.

When I hoisted myself out of the pool and pattered down the concrete in my dripping swimsuit, I couldn't help being drawn to the wonderfully tanned girl at the concession center, who kept pivoting in her yellow bikini, bobbing to the music as she took orders. I gave her a quarter and grinned as she mixed up a "Suicide," blonde hair swaying while she shifted from the Coke dispenser to the Dr. Pepper and root beer. I could hear Bachman-Turner Overdrive belting out "You Ain't Seen Nothing Yet," and it was all exciting in a new, male way. To be fourteen going on fifteen. To feel that anything was possible. And to be here in small-town America with a personal connection to a huge panoramic cause on the other side of the globe.

In Ethiopia, rebel soldiers had rounded up all parliamentary representatives and civil servants, labeling them "Enemies of the Revolution." Then they had dragged fifty-seven of these prominent leaders out of the basement of the Palace of Menelik, transporting them to the main prison and machine-gunning them as they stepped from the trucks. The newspapers were suggesting that the shadowy new leaders might be in league with our arch enemies, the Soviets. Mom and Dad were hearing reports of Christians being singled out, told to recant or suffer the consequences. They said an Ethiopian doctor at one of the mission hospitals had been forced to walk to jail nearly naked and barefoot, with men shooting rifles into the air. Why? Simply because he was associated with Americans and their foreign religion.

As the lead singer for Bachman-Turner Overdrive stuttered out his signature "B-b-b-baby," I was struck that somewhere, right now, there might be people I had actually touched who were in prison for what they believed. I knew I should be grieving like my parents, but in all honesty I found it exciting. There was a strange appeal to the situation—the allure of being part of something bigger than myself, something meaningful like the huge novel by Alexandre Dumas, which I had been reading that summer. Over there in Ethiopia, real people were living lives just as dramatic as Dantès in *The Count of Monte Cristo*, being imprisoned wrongfully and hoping to escape—to get revenge or, at least, see that God balanced the equation. And to my surprise, that seemed inviting.

Four

’m back again—the intrusive older guy. Yes, missionaries are driven by a desire to spread their faith; however, they are also driven to have adventure. Although they may not admit it, many of them have an instinctive attraction to danger—a desire to live life in a large risky way, going beyond where others would stop.

The most famous missionary associated with Africa, Dr. David Livingstone, became well known in the 1850s when he did what no white man had done before, walking his way clear across southern Africa, where he eventually discovered the great Zambezi falls of Mosi-oa-Tunya ("Smoke that Thunders") on the border of present-day Zimbabwe. Having been hailed by the Royal Geographic Society, he left the employ of the London Missionary Society to lead a subsequent expedition searching for the source of the Nile. He felt sure that such exploration fit into his missionary mandate since it would open the Nile to river traffic, which would allow for the spread of Christianity and hopefully force an end to the ruthless Arab slave trade.

Although Livingstone never did identify the head of the Nile—despite wandering off the known map for six years—he did explore the great lakes of Tanganyika and Malawi and Bangweulu. And when he died, debilitated by malaria and dysentery, he was a thousand miles from the port where he began. According to legend, his body was found kneeling by his cot in a praying posture and the local tribe would not allow his porters to carry the corpse away until they had removed the heart, insisting, "You can have his body, but his heart belongs in Africa."

That was in 1873, and only twenty years later, the founder of my parents' mission—Rowland Bingham—started his own exploratory journeys, no doubt very aware of Livingstone, whose remains were carried to the coast of Zanzibar before being shipped to Britain for burial at Westminster Abbey. Bingham, a British-born Canadian, made a very Livingstonian proclamation, "I will open Africa to the gospel or die trying," and though he didn't end up dying, he got awfully close. Starting from the coast of present-day Nigeria, he hiked into the vast interior, turning back only when one companion died of malaria and another succumbed after a period of captivity. On a second attempt, Bingham himself nearly died from malaria. It was only when he had recruited four new missionaries from Canada that he was able to establish the first station of the Sudan Interior Mission, four hundred miles inland, where yet another recruit died and two had to return home, broken by illness.

Still, Bingham lived on, directing the growing mission through World War I, eventually handing on the pioneering baton to hundreds of inspired recruits, including an American named Malcolm Forsberg, who, in 1934, rode a mule several hundred miles into the southernmost mountains of Ethiopia, living in a thatched hut until he could marry his fiancée and bring her to join him. And it was this intrepid couple, perhaps the first white foreigners to see whole valleys and mountainsides of an unreached region, who trained my parents at mission candidate school in New York City in 1964.

Malcolm and Enid Forsberg were cheerful, enthusiastic retirees by the time my parents met them, yet they were still raising the flag, so to speak, and sending new recruits right back into the fire, despite having been forced out of Ethiopia by the Italian occupation and having left neighboring Sudan due to civil war—which is to say that my parents came by their risk-taking exploratory hankering in an honest way, even if they themselves didn't recognize how much it motivated them. By joining Sudan Interior Mission in the 1960s, they became part of a Religious Geographic Society not unlike the Royal Geographic Society, determined to reach "the ends of the earth" but for different reasons. A pioneer-like love of adventure went naturally with their sense of mission. They had something large to accomplish, and since they felt "called" by God, anything they attempted would be worth the risk.

This, of course, is the exact mentality necessary for serious expeditionary work—the willingness to risk death for the sake of something more important. Paradoxically, the one who commits to such ventures tends to think that risking death is worth the stress because out there, on the verge of annihilation, is where life might be found. Hadn't Jesus himself said, "The man who loves his life will lose it, while the man who hates his life in this world will keep it for eternal life"?

Such was the gung-ho mentality of my parents as they "signed on" with the Sudan Interior Mission. And such was the mentality of a whole slew of other missionaries I got to know as a child, including an older mission couple who came to visit our house in Kansas just as I was beginning ninth grade: a couple named Doris and Nathan Barlow.

Five

wenty years older than my parents, the Barlows were true mission veterans. They were some of the first to reenter Ethiopia after the Italian occupation of World War II. In 1946 they helped to reestablish the very first SIM mission station at Soddo in Wolaitta district, staying and working in the area. Aunt Doris, as we called her, had helped Mom to keep house when we arrived in the 1960s, explaining that eucalyptus branches could be set down around the edge of a room to deter invading ants, and that the sugar bowl should be kept in a plate of water to protect it from insect marauders. Meanwhile, Dr. Barlow had coached my father, introducing him to the exotic diseases he would have to diagnose: not just the swollen necks of goiter, but the huge scaly legs of elephantiasis or the sickening scent of fistula.

The two of them, both over sixty, were thin, immaculate people who wore simple un-patterned shirts with clean white Keds on their feet. Their silver hair had a kind of bright suddenness next to their ruddy faces. They seemed a paired team in every way except one: Dr. Barlow had a glass eye. He had lost his vision in one eye just like my father, who was blinded on one side all the way back in high school, when a fleck ricocheted from a bullet at a firing range.

Dad still had his real eye, which drifted a little, but Dr. Barlow's glass eye always seemed quite off-kilter, as if noticing something I had missed. The moment he stepped into our house at Troy, the sight of him brought back the smell of the Soddo hospital when I was only three years old—all ammonia and alcohol and purple antiseptic. It brought back barefoot workmen stomping in a mud pit beside the hospital, throwing in straw and dung to make adobe. And Marta, our housekeeper, with a tub full of wet clothes, smacking the wet fabric on the washboard while humming hymns.

Then I began remembering a whole queue of other people, a host of lost aunts and uncles: the nurses and doctors and builders and pilots and ministers and schoolteachers who had lived with us as part of the Sudan Interior Mission, all good sturdy Christian folk, full of moral purpose and the cheerful refusal to think negatively. A large and zealous family united by allegiance to the same spiritual cause.

On the second day of the Barlows' visit, a Saturday, I came down the steps at 9:00, having overslept, and I was transported by the exuberant vigor of these two tough veterans moving around our kitchen, blowing at their coffee mugs. They had walked five miles, starting a bit after sunrise, and they teased me about going back out with them. The sight of them in our kitchen, so full of positive energy, created a strange ambivalence. No longer was Ethiopia an abstract notion. To admit my attraction toward them was to risk being drawn right back into the reality of that other world.

"I hear you're becoming quite a speller," Dr. Barlow said, and I nodded.

"Okay, then, I've got a word for you. It's a ten-dollar word. A real doozy. Are you ready?"

I nodded again.

"How do you spell 'sanctification'?"

"Nathan!" exclaimed his wife, but I grinned. Although he was talking to me like I was ten instead of fourteen, I didn't mind. I enjoyed the challenge. This was a piece of cake, since I had seen it at church a hundred times.

"Very impressive," he said after I had finished. "Now how about a trickier one? 'Apostle.'"

I spelled it without a hitch and stayed amused as Dr. Barlow kept quizzing me, but once he swung his attention back to my parents, I felt a shadow of apprehension as if a cloud passed overhead. I noticed the intense way that Mom and Dad asked about people back in Ethiopia, wanting to know whether Marta, our maid, was okay despite all the crackdowns on Christian "sympathizers." They wanted to know, too, whether he had seen Nana the evangelist.

"Fine, fine. Nana is still making his journeys into the Mursi area, even though there is a warrant for his arrest."

"And what about Waja?" Mom asked. "Has there been any word from prison? Any chance of a release?"

One of the more upsetting tales that had come back to us from Ethiopia was that of Waja, a physician's assistant whom we had known when he was being trained at our station in Wolaitta. After completing his training, he had traveled south and west, away from the immense open savannah of the Rift Valley and into a smaller adjoining valley where he could establish a pharmacy, serving people in a poor rival tribe. Apparently, his determined kindness gained him enemies because his pharmacy was raided by jealous cadres who took all the medications from the shelves and dragged him into court as an antirevolutionary. They had no resistance from the judge as they applied Marx's oft-quoted criticism that "religion . . . is the opium of the people"—a tool used by imperialists to keep everyone docile. The accusers mocked Waja for his beliefs, and in reaction he lifted his shackles, calling out, "Don't you know? This is like getting a hero's medal. I have received a decoration for Jesus."

For his apparent contempt, the nervous judge sentenced him to a notorious forced-labor camp, where he would have to dig trenches and carry rocks with no date of release. No one was able to contact him until his wife got permission to bring food. Dr. Barlow explained: "She says the guards have chosen him as the doctor for all prisoners. Can you believe that?"

"Absolutely!" my father said. "I had only one problem with Waja. He was too competent. Too handsome, too. In fact, it made him hard to stand next to!"

Dr. Barlow chuckled. "He definitely did good work."

"Maybe that's because you trained him."

Dr. Barlow smiled more softly, his good eye fixed on Dad while his glass eye looked somewhere else. He seemed embarrassed by my father's compliment, not sure what to do with it.

"You know what?" Dad added. "You ought to tell the boys about your hernia operation. Didn't you use it as a practice case for one of the dressers?"

"That was the idea," said Dr. Barlow.

"Boys," said Dad, "what do you think? Could you show someone how to operate on you, especially if the person had never done an operation?"

We were hooked. I leaped in, "You mean you stayed awake and showed him where to cut?"

Dr. Barlow's good eye crinkled at the corner as he turned toward me. "Yup. Had to use a mirror."

Now that he was properly warmed, Dad didn't have to coax Dr. Barlow into telling how he had lain there on the operating table, calming the anxious dresser as he pointed out where to cut and how to stitch.

"Watch out for the femoral artery," Dad joked. "No pressure, of course, but you don't want to nick that one. Now let's see, in a mirror everything's reversed. So would that be right, or left?"

We all laughed big belly laughs. I knew that Dr. Barlow and Aunt Doris were to be admired because of the respectful way my parents spoke of them. Yes, their gentle teasing and insistent cheerfulness grated on me sometimes, perhaps because I felt, like my father, that they were hard to stand next to. And yes, there was a kind of severity to their goodness, which seemed so disciplined, so dutiful, that it was almost soldierly. But who was I to question Christians of such high caliber? Selfless. Caring. Boldly faithful.

When at last they got into their Ford sedan, I was sad in an old way—sweet and nostalgic and deeply melancholic—as if our family lived on a remote island and our only guests were sailing away. Their presence had brought Ethiopia back in a manner that was more than mere memory. I was torn. Part of me wanted to get in the car and go with them, while another part was reminded of the sacrifices required. After all, I had not forgotten what it felt like to be a seven-year-old at boarding school in Addis—small and inadequate next to the biblical model that kept coming up in chapel: David, the warrior-youth, who had willingly left home to go off and kill a giant with his sling.

On the night after the Barlows left, I lay awake a long time, unable to sleep. For a bit, I tried counting backward from one hundred. Then I fell to spelling, tackling whatever words came to mind. I spelled them out as they occurred to me: Sanctification. Apostle. Physician. Surgery. Laceration. Humor. Holiness. Martyrdom. Anxiety.

When at last I dozed off, I dreamed that I was in a Land Rover with my father and he was asking if I felt ready to return to boarding school. We hurtled down a rocky road, knocking aside goats and chickens that lingered too long, and when he asked again, "Are you ready," I could only say yes because I knew that I should be willing to do what was right, what might be God's will. After all, true Christians were not afraid to go wherever God called them.

Six

I had a dream while revising this book for the third or fourth time, and in the dream I was completely naked.

As I recall, I had been worrying about whether my story, with all its Christian references, would appeal only to religious readers. Those worries, triggered by a comment from a literary agent, had created a humiliating sense that I belonged back in the ghetto with all the others of my kind, which is exactly where I found myself in this buck-naked dream: back at the conservative Christian college I attended after high school in Africa, an intense evangelical pocket of idealistic Christians in the secular sprawl of Chicago.

Wheaton College, famous for its globe-trotting evangelist Billy Graham, was a center for much of the American evangelical missionary movement in the 1900s. Another famed alumnus, the missionary Jim Elliot, had been martyred by a Stone Age tribe in the jungles of Ecuador, and people were still quoting from his college journal: "He is no fool who gives what he cannot keep to gain that which he cannot lose."

Anyway, in the dream I was twenty years old and back at Wheaton. However, I was standing around naked and, strangely enough, feeling good about it, quite natural really, despite the fact that I was in the middle of a small party on one of the lawns outside a limestone administration building. Everyone was sipping soda or punch. (No wine at Wheaton, since we had all signed a pledge to refrain from alcohol, tobacco, dancing, and sex.) And I saw a professorial man in the crowd who clearly had to be Ethiopian.

His eyes were creased at the corners in a fine, wise fashion. "Tenahstehlin," I said to him, trying out a traditional greeting, and he lit up, acknowledging that he spoke Amharic and had indeed lived most his life in Ethiopia, though he was born in Egypt originally.

I tried next to say something complicated in Amharic, but after several failed attempts, I took my hands off my naked hips and, borrowing a red pen, began to write whole sentences across my lower abdomen. It seemed the most logical way to clarify, and he followed along comfortably, tilting his head to read phrases, then smiling and nodding. However, his attention to the hasty scrawl on my belly began to make me feel odd. The words, so bright scarlet on my stomach, made me wonder how I might appear to others. No one else was writing on their skin, so I stopped. I was overcome with the need to cover what I had written, so I swiped a couple blank sheets of paper off a table and taped them around my waist like a wide white belt.

As you might imagine, this peculiar attempt to cover up only made me more self-conscious. I became aware, for the first time, of my genitals poking out from beneath the white band. What must others think, I wondered. After all, none of them were standing in the buff. So I tugged this paper belt lower like a kind of mini-dress, only to feel it tear apart. Suddenly I was wretchedly aware of my exposed self— the black pubic hair and fleshy thumb of my penis, the too-white buttocks that everyone could see from behind.

I had not felt at all uneasy while talking with the Ethiopian professor, but my body had become aflame with shame now, as if lit with neon from inside. I turned and scampered toward a dorm, trying to hold the torn paper over crucial areas. I ran up three flights of stairs with girls coming down past me, averting their eyes or acting as if this was all quite normal. Then on the last flight, I realized I was in the wrong dorm altogether: the girls' dorm. I stood trapped before an all-white door and waited for I knew not what.

It would seem that, by telling the true underlying story of my life (even the parts I might be inclined to hide beneath a neat clean story line), I risk angering the people of my youth, my parents too. Yet I know that by not telling that naked narrative, I risk losing trust. As a result, even though I fear becoming a laughingstock, here I stand. Me. The boy who was raised in a zealous, evangelical Christian family—part of a subculture that the Marxists have always found foolish. Me. The older man who wants to distance himself from that religious child, becoming smarter than his parents or the others who shaped him. Me. Who must admit that, in fact, I am probably no wiser than they are and certainly less admirable.

Seven

y parents received a letter from the director of our former mission, describing the critical need for medical workers, most of whom had transferred out of the country, alarmed by worsening conditions. I noticed that my parents replied to the director and sent a mass mailing to former supporters listing "Urgent Prayer Requests." And because they were becoming more focused on our former home country, I became more focused. I began to send a few letters of my own, addressing them to old classmates at Bingham Academy, such as Danny Coleman, who had been my closest friend in grade school. Still, I was surprised when I got an actual reply from this long-removed friend, who fondly recalled how we had pretended to be frontier heroes like Daniel Boone, trading marbles through the fence to get "victuals" from passing Ethiopian boys, usually in the form of sugar cane.

I was also surprised to receive a blue aerogram from Mari Dye, a girl who had lived on the compound of our second station. She and her sisters had played with my brother and me during holidays, joining our backyard Olympics when we pole-vaulted with bamboo poles and rode sticks over steeplechase obstacles. In third grade, just before we came back to the United States, she had briefly agreed to be my "girlfriend," hiding with me under the pines at Bingham Academy so that we could hold hands and swap candy. Now she lived at our first station, Soddo—the same place where we had met the Barlows—and she had enclosed a picture of herself.

I felt an immediate déjà vu as I scanned the background of that photo, noting the corner of a house with green-painted tin and heavily shadowed eaves. I wondered if it might be the very house I had lived in as a toddler. I was nearly positive I had seen that whitewashed

corner a thousand times and that, if I could go around it, I would discover a steel barrel that caught runoff water from the roof, storing it
for the dry season.

I stared even more closely at Mari. She had changed so much—no
longer wearing the pointy glasses that I recalled, no longer thin and
gangly but filled out in pleasant ways. Although she had her frank
mischievous grin, she was not exactly a girl anymore, and this made
me realize I was no longer simply a boy.

In the letter, Mari had the usual teenage things to talk about: other
kids I might remember, soccer games, pet rabbits, and so forth. My
parents told me, however, that life at Soddo, where her father was
acting station manager, had been completely altered by the revolution. A high school there, which was administered by the mission, had
become a target for local communist leaders. Even some of the Ethiopian staff had helped to organize a student strike after listening to
government radio broadcasts. Apparently, they were convinced that
the missionaries were secret agents trying to dupe them in a scheme
to keep Africans in economic slavery. One teacher had even confronted the mission administrator on an empty path, threatening to
kill him and his wife if they didn't leave.

When I looked at that photo of Mari Dye pinned to a bulletin board
in my room, I felt a mix of confused emotions. Attraction. Nostalgia.
Fear. Indignation. It was strange to think that she was so far away yet
standing where I had once stood. It was strange to think of the things
she might be experiencing and how that might be changing her. What
was it like to see the words "Go Home Yankee" scrawled on the hospital wall? To know that the students at the school for the blind were
wrapping their faces with bandanas because they had been told the
missionaries were trying to infect them with tuberculosis?

Years later, during college courses on colonialism, I would begin to
understand the basis of the Marxist critique of missionaries. I would
realize how, whether we liked it or not, our organization was part of
the pro-capitalist alliance that had developed between Hailie Selassie
and major Western nations. Ever since Dr. Lambie—the first member of our mission to reach Ethiopia—agreed to the emperor's request for a hospital in Addis Ababa, Sudan Interior Mission had become linked to the emperor and his network of aristocrats. We were
treated as a privileged part of his plan for development, so we were

sometimes resented. In areas where local tribes had no option but to sharecrop on land owned by the emperor's tribe, we could look a bit too special, given free land and praised by visiting officials.

I can see all that now. However, at the time, I had only a gut reaction. When I stared at the photo of Mari Dye standing in front of a house that had once been mine, I was overcome by a kind of sad outrage. Something warrior-like began to rise up in me. Yes, it would be frightening to live in a place like that—like walking into a fire. Yet I couldn't help feeling drawn to the defense of those who seemed unfairly judged: not only Western missionaries who were being harassed but even more so the local Christians who were getting jailed and beaten. Why should they, simply because of their association with the mission, be subjected to wrath?

Now fifteen, I had a desire to prove myself—to be tested and to show myself worthy. I was not fully surprised, as a result, by what happened next. It seemed fated, if you will—or ordained by God.

As I wrapped up my freshman year at Troy High School and as my older brother learned that he had been accepted to attend the college I would eventually attend—Wheaton College—Dad called us into the living room for a family conference. He said he had received a letter from the director of Sudan Interior Mission asking, quite clearly, whether we would return to Ethiopia. He wanted to know if we were willing to consider that possibility.

Mom stayed quiet as Dad explained. Nat's eyes widened. Johnathan turned pale.

Dad said that, due to the ongoing revolution, the mission had lost almost all its medical staff. Now the only doctor in Addis Ababa was leaving on furlough, so a replacement was needed.

"Does this mean we're going back?" I asked.

"Nothing's decided. The Ethiopian government is denying visas, so it might not even be possible. It's an opportunity, that's all. . . ."

"Do you want to go?" asked Johnathan, who looked queasy under his brown tumble of hair, no longer my bossy big brother but almost toddler-like in his vulnerability. I could see the divot-like scar on his cheek where Mom said the forceps had cut him during childbirth, and I was struck that if we went, he would probably not go with us. He would be left here alone at college, just like he had been left alone at boarding school four years before me—as a first grader.

"Well there's a need, and we like to go where we're needed. Everyone may have to leave soon, so this could be the last chance to go in and do what's possible."

I could hear the eagerness under my father's noncommittal response. The way he said "go in" sounded like a beach landing on D-Day or a paratrooper strike. There was a kind of dramatic urgency to it: "Your mission, should you choose to accept it. . . ."

"So how long before we leave?" I asked, testing to see just how settled this plan might be.

Mom interrupted, "We won't go unless the family agrees. It's something to pray about, that's all."

This was the summer of 1976, the Bicentennial of the United States, which only made our secret family plan more dramatic and alluring. Troy had caught the patriotic fever sweeping the nation. On July 4th, the two-hundredth birthday of the nation, we all went down to the county courthouse. I wasn't thinking consciously about the politics of my parents' imminent decision, but I felt it in my bones. The Iron Curtain was still an ominous fixture in Cold War Europe, and I tended to imagine a dark communist shadow hovering over the northeast quadrant of the map, threatening to ooze out onto places like Ethiopia. To go right into that darkness, hoping to push it back, was frightening, yet it made me feel as if I could do something that really mattered. As I took my place in the summer band, playing trumpet in the brass section next to Dad and Johnathan, I became suddenly nostalgic— keenly aware that there was a very real chance this would be my last time in the band, my last time on the town square, my last time to be the Kansas boy I had become here in this community.

We all sat on folding chairs on the grass, wet at the armpits. We played "Yankee Doodle Dandy" and "Stars and Stripes Forever." We played "America the Beautiful." Then we got up and joined the long line that led to tables of pies made from recipes passed down generation to generation.

One of the ladies serving at the checkered table of the Troy Pollyana Club was Bertie Hamilton, virtually the only black person in the whole town and a very loyal member of our church, Troy First

Baptist. Bertie, who was an eighty-five-year-old with caramel-colored skin and a halo of silver hair, made the best dessert at every church potluck, a peach cobbler that seemed to be all song and sunshine. I also happened to know that Bertie was the daughter of a woman who was actually born into slavery before the Civil War. For me, as a naive Kansas teen on July 4th, she was living proof, in this sense, that history could be corrected.

There she stood, behind the checkered tablecloth in her favorite pink skirt and white patent-leather sandals, spooning dollops of vanilla ice cream onto the plates while her forehead and upper lip glistened. And after she handed me a serving of her famous cobbler, winking at the extra ice cream she added, I savored not only the burst of peach-and-cream flavor that came with my first forkful, but the sheer Americanness of it all: flags in the wind, sun lowering on the horizon, trumpets on the lawn. I was proud to just be here—a member of a nation that had lasted two hundred years, a nation that had weathered its own civil war to get rid of slavery. I was optimistic about justice and change. No, the United States was not perfect, but I was a fifteen-year-old surrounded by patriotic bunting and martial music, and I felt a euphoric sense that I, even I, could make a difference.

Eight

t can be difficult to think about the past through the lens of the present: like crossing your eyes and seeing double. When you are five or ten or even fifteen, the world is not refracted like that, bent through all the accumulated layers of history. Everything is right there in front of you and wonderfully straightforward, sharply defined even to the point of pain, but not complicated.

Which is why the first time I wrote this book, it was a pleasure to go back to an early, simple way of seeing, allowing myself to be a teenager again. I didn't want to step away and introduce the prism of retrospection like I'm doing here, which forces me to look at the most vivid months of my life through a sort of befuddling bifocal or trifocal.

Here's the thing: everything has a context, if not a hundred contexts. We just don't realize that when we are young, at least I didn't. In 1977, as my parents started talking about taking us into a Marxist revolution, I couldn't see beyond the singular notion that Karl Marx was a bad guy with a big beard (bad, I say, because he was an atheist, which you couldn't trump for badness, since it was a rejection of the most fundamental truth my family claimed).

Since I associated Marx with the Soviets in northern Europe, who were still a very real political power, I had no idea who Marx actually was. I had no idea that he had died long before the Russian revolution—even before my grandfather was born. Or that he had worked as a journalist in London, which went against my assumption that he ran around with a rifle, leading rebel charges.

Here, though, is what I know now. In 1867 Karl Marx published the first volume of *Das Kapital* and began writing quietly on the second and third volumes, no doubt very aware of the famous British missionary David Livingstone, who was trying to open the interior of Africa. Marx must have known about Livingstone because by then he was already in London, having been thrown out of Belgium and France after publishing his *Communist Manifesto*. So there he sat, an obsessive researcher in the British Museum Library, taking all his free time to dig through stacks of books about the capitalistic ventures of Europe while this renowned missionary explorer became the toast of the town, pictured as a true Christian and patriot. It seemed that not only was Dr. Livingstone risking everything to learn about the headwaters of the Nile, but he was doing it kindly—with a small crew of porters, befriending natives, sending back impassioned pleas for England to get involved immediately so as to stop the cruelties of Arab slave traders.

Marx was still there in London, watching as newspapers reported Livingstone's legendary death and as the body was brought back from Zanzibar to Westminster Abbey. He was still at the heart of the empire working on the same economic theories, probably with not a clue how profoundly those theories would reconfigure the world map. And I wonder what he was thinking as he heard this Christian hero lionized. What exactly was going through his mind as English politicians and businessmen began to imagine a new set of untapped resources that might be more lucrative than the ones in familiar Asia and the Middle East? What did he mutter as those colonists speculated about English commerce and civilization in Africa—the possibility of vast farms and mining operations, not to mention whole tribes of savages turned to "proper" moral conduct?

Today, I can't help hearing ironic resonances in lines such as this from his three-volume *Das Kapital*: "Capitalist production, therefore, develops technology and the combining together of various processes into a social whole, only by sapping the original sources of all wealth—the soil and the laborer." Or this even more pithy maxim that spilled from his pen: "The road to Hell is paved with good intentions."

At the time of Livingstone's death in 1873, Europe controlled not even 10 percent of the African continent, but that percentage would grow exponentially by Marx's death in 1883, and within another thirty years the only two areas not colonized would be Liberia (which hardly counts because former slaves had been allowed to start a self-governed state) and Ethiopia (where a very astute ruler, King Menelik, had amassed an army of 100,000, defeating well-equipped Italian troops and proving that African warriors could repel a colonial land grab). As for England, by the beginning of World War I, it controlled not only South Africa and Rhodesia and Nigeria, but Ethiopia's neighbors, Sudan and Kenya, plus Uganda, Egypt, and Tanzania. It also had become so invested in the potential resources of East Africa that it was financing the transport of 32,000 Indian coolies to build, upon their weary backs, a rail line all the way from the coastal town of Mombasa to a spot on the shores of Lake Victoria close to the fabled headwaters Livingstone had sought.

If Marx had lived long enough to see that absurdly expensive railroad built by an imported working class at the cost of £5 million and 2,500 deaths, or if he had watched the merchants of England begin to tally their imagined profits from distant tea and coffee plantations, I imagine his eyes would have burned in their sockets. Nor would he have looked kindly upon the quickly expanding Christian church, which he had always argued was a tool used by capitalists to subdue the working class, an opiate that pacified them by shifting their attention from current justice to future heavenly rewards.

By 1914, English-speaking Protestant missionaries had established settlements in all the British-held regions of Africa, reaching even remote villages like Nasir on the southeastern edge of Sudan, where young Dr. Lambie, soon to be the first Sudan interior missionary in Ethiopia, established a new station after traveling up the Nile from Egypt as Livingstone had anticipated. To get that close to the Ethiopian border, Lambie had turned east on a tributary of the Nile and waited for rains to float the grounded steamboat. In places the crew was forced to dig new channels or drag the beached boat forward by its anchor ropes. Nevertheless, Lambie refused to be discouraged. He had tremendous respect for the British military who governed Sudan, and he lavished praise on a general who had died showing martyr-like resolve: "Would that we missionaries could show a like heroism and unselfishness."

In actuality, it was due to this sort of soldierly commitment that missionaries kept reaching farther and farther into the remotest corners of Africa, winning disciples in increasing numbers. And had Marx lived to see that era, probably grinding his teeth in reaction, he would have also cheered for one surprisingly tough underdog. Ethiopia alone seemed to be foiling the reach of Western nations. Marx would have approved without perhaps realizing that, even as Ethiopia fought off the Christian imperialism of Europe, it was subject to its own Christian imperialism, ejecting all missionaries unless they converted to the ancient Orthodox Christianity of the ruling tribe, the Amharas. It was a monarchy built upon a very religious foundation, so religious that no king or queen could be crowned without the blessing of the head patriarch, who would grant the ruler this most imposing title: "Elect of God."

What finally created a new openness for Western missionaries in Ethiopia was a second Italian invasion at the outset of World War II, when Mussolini's well-equipped troops used aerial bombardment and mustard gas to drive their way into the capital of Addis, forcing the new emperor, Hailie Selassie, into exile. Alarmed, England came to the emperor's assistance and helped to march him back into his territory, and with his triumphant return, a new alliance was forged. Realizing that he was part of a new world order, Hailie Selassie decided at last to open his doors to Protestant missions like Sudan Interior Mission.

The emperor knew, of course, that his own ruling tribe was predominantly Orthodox and that he owed his power to that church, so he told the arriving missionaries they were prohibited from evangelizing throughout the northern highlands, stronghold of the Ethiopian aristocracy. They could proselytize only in the less-developed regions of the south, where the peasant class observed animist traditions or Islam. That was fine apparently because with the missionaries would come schools and hospitals, books and airplanes, roads and new farming techniques.

So the gates swung open and in surged a new set of recruits, including my parents eventually, with me in tow—a mere three years old and primarily interested in chameleons and poinsettias and baboons, as opposed to colonial politics.

Nine

welve years had passed since our first entry into Ethiopia, and here we were again, knocking on the door. Only this time, the country had reverted to its former isolationist stance, suspicious of all Western influences except the ideas of a certain nineteenth-century Prussian—Karl Marx.

July gave way to August, and the Ethiopian consulate still had not approved our visas. Then August passed, and Johnathan went off to his first year of college while Nat and I reenrolled at the Troy schools.

Another month passed, and the Barlows made a quick visit, trying to assure us that the visas would be approved eventually. "They're blocking Westerners, but they're not going to turn down a doctor. Besides, everyone is praying."

So I prayed too. I wanted to be as faithful as the Barlows—wanted to believe prayers really could be answered. I prayed that God would cause the officials at the consulate to approve our visas even if it went counter to their no-missionary policy. If we were approved, it would be a sign. I'd take it as a sign, I told God. And to show how much faith I had, I started to prepare. I checked out a library book on auto repairs. I figured that since we might be driving hundreds of miles from the nearest mechanic, I ought to know how to replace a fan belt or bleed a brake line. I also checked out another very practical book, a survival manual titled *Bushcraft*, and began to study how to set snares with trip wires, how to gut animals, how to start a fire with flint or friction.

Eventually Thanksgiving drew near, and the sheer passage of time wore me down. I returned the overdue library books and paid the fees. I began to envision what it might be like to simply stay and finish my sophomore year. Maybe we weren't supposed to go at all . . .

except that one evening at supper Mom and Dad opened an envelope from the Ethiopian consulate and announced that the visas had been approved.

I remember feeling shaken. I had slacked in my commitment. Would God find me worthy? Would my waffling jeopardize everything?

I was pulled out of my introspection only after Mom murmured, "Of course, there's your Grandmother Conrad. We're not sure what arrangements need to be made for her."

Uh oh. Grandma!

Again I remembered the flash of alarm that had come into her eyes each time my parents talked about the Barlows visiting, and the sad wistfulness that settled over her when my mother brought up the loss of medical staff in Ethiopia. It was unsettling to watch Grandma's eyes go soft and liquid behind their magnifying lenses, skipping from her daughter's face to her son-in-law's. So now I felt foreboding. What effect would this news have on her, with her decades of heart trouble and nitroglycerin pills?

As it turned out, the impact was devastating. Two days after Mom confirmed that we were going to leave, Grandmother had a stroke. She was comatose for a week, and when she came to, she didn't recognize any of us.

With that disastrous twist, departing suddenly became very complicated. Although Grandmother Conrad was able to sit up after several weeks and started to recognize Mom, there was no way to simply leave her in such condition. It became necessary for Dad, Nat, and me to fly out of the country without Mom, assuming that eventually she would nurse her mother to health and follow us.

After a sparse Christmas celebration in a nearly empty house, we said good-bye to brother Johnathan, who had arranged a ride to college and left with a fragile smile. Then we squeezed two bulging footlockers and a suitcase into the trunk of our tiny Chevette. Neighbors and friends had come to say good-bye, and they stood on the lawn, huffing in the frigid air. After Pastor Leroy led the group in prayer, Dad pulled us into a circle with everyone looping arms over shoulders. He wouldn't let us out of this ring until we had sung "They Will Know We Are Christians by Our Love," sidling and step-kicking as if we were Greeks at a wedding. Everyone was laughing as he slammed the hatch down on the Chevette, causing the entire back window to explode. More laughter—and consternation. Then a decision to just drive the car anyway.

Riding to Kansas City in that chilled Chevette felt so ludicrously normal that it was hard for me to imagine we were really doing anything more unusual than going to a repair shop. With all of us shouting over the blasts of cold air in the broken hatch, and with trucks ripping by in the other lane, it was hard for me to believe that any realm could exist other than this very cold, very windy place on the highway in Kansas.

Then we arrived at the airport, where Mom would have to say good-bye, and the finality of it all settled in. She patted her chest, wiping away silent tears. I could tell she hated having to stay behind while we headed to Ethiopia. Still, Nat and I hugged her—followed by my father—and we all three filed down the metal tunnel into the plane. With our takeoff, Kansas became the abstract place in my mind instead of Ethiopia. The town of Troy became an unreachable memory, locked into the receding time line of my past.

Ten

We live in space and time, and just as I cannot be in two places at one time, I cannot be in two times at one place. Except in my mind, which is the amazing reality-warping machine that leaps me out of a current January day to a January day thirty-seven years earlier, and from my home in Iowa to the sky over the Atlantic Ocean back when Trans World Airlines still existed with its catchy advertising jingle: "Up, up, and away, with TWA."

My mind does all that space and time travel from a white leather couch in my living room, where I am longing for something that can only be remembered, not reentered. Whether I like it or not, I am half a century old and living in a different world. I know this, and I also know that I should be thankful for the security that allows me to live past the average life expectancy in most countries. Yet when I look at the morning newspaper, I must admit some secret, even perverse attraction to the places pictured, where young protesters or rebel soldiers seem caught up in a more dramatic existence.

In Syria, where the government has shelled a university, killing eighty-two students, rebels are blasting holes in walls to create corridors safe from snipers. In Pakistan, where a girl was dragged off a school bus and shot for making a public comment about the need for women's education, her classmates are nervously riding the bus again, wondering who might get targeted. Death looms around each corner, along with the threat of pain. But I can't help imagining that the pictured people, even in their suffering, are acutely aware of being alive—which seems better, in some sense, than living forever and never knowing I am alive.

Isn't this, at a subconscious level, why we, as Americans, have such an appetite for action-adventure films, many of them about apocalypse? Aren't we secretly wishing we lived lives that were larger, more intense, more truly meaningful than the ones we actually live?

When we have a cause, we live for a reason. We also do our living in relation to others who share the same purpose, so we have a community of solidarity. At some level, if we are honest, we may even feel too vital to die, at least not until we have accomplished what we are trying to accomplish. Since we are part of a greater plan, the plan itself is protection.

Ridiculous, you may say, but that is how I was geared as a teenager back in 1977, as my father, my brother, and I winged our way east and south toward Ethiopia, swinging down along the rim of the huge USSR and its empire of satellite nations, which were cordoned off by a "Curtain" that was hard not to imagine as some sort of cloud-high sheet, rigid and black and dangling from a gigantic rod, keeping us out, or was it them in? Even though I am older and quite aware now of the damage done by such us-or-them definitions, and even though I'm thankful to wake up "safe" these days, I can't help feeling a strange nostalgia for that youthful time when I felt so confident of who was right and who was wrong, almost eager to hear the challenging whisper in my head: "Go ahead, risk everything."

Eleven

orty-eight hours flew by in an airport flurry. After stops in New York and London, I finally succumbed to my own fatigue. Somewhere over Egypt, I fell asleep, befuddled by all the changes in time zones. When I woke, I was completely disoriented. I looked out the window to see the mountains of Ethiopia rising underneath me, feeling a strange sensation of having been here before. Was I fifteen or nine? Coming or going?

The ground came up to meet me like a companion I had left just the day before. There were the same familiar ridges and threadbare patches of grass that I had looked down upon when I was flying into Addis on board a DC-3 to begin third grade. And no doubt those were the same clusters of half-rusted tin roofs I had seen, draped with a gray haze of eucalyptus smoke. I also recognized a row of blue taxicabs rattling toward the airport, and a line of donkeys trotting in their distinctive knee-popping way, half-buried under loads of hay. Then the plane skipped and roared, slowed on the runway, and the scene outside my window lost all this déjà vu magic, blocked by a giant olive-green cargo plane with a red Soviet flag on its tail.

Inside the airport everything seemed radically altered. A renovation project had stopped mid-progress, with untiled cement everywhere and draped plastic along the corridors. Soldiers slouched against the unfinished walls, wiry brown, smoky-eyed, sullen. Machine guns swung from straps around their necks, and they rested their forearms on the barrels as if wearing slings. They didn't seem to care if the weapons pointed straight at us.

Clearly, this was no longer the emperor's elite welcome pad with its swanky, second-floor restaurant and courteous officials. If we had any doubts about the new leanings of the government, they disappeared as we rode into Addis with the missionary who picked us up. When we got to Meskel Square, or Square of the Cross, it was no longer recognizable, having been changed into Revolution Square with an immense scarlet billboard hovering over it. Even I—with my limited, teenage sense of history—recognized the portraits on the blood-bright board: Marx, Engel, and Lenin. Paradoxically Caucasian, these political giants stared down at us like a deified triumvirate, super-sized gods in a brave new world. They were the rescuing heroes. The saviors of the oppressed. And though we were foreigners like them, we were now opposite to them. Enemies of the state.

The anti-American sentiment in Addis Ababa was not subtle. We passed another billboard near Red Square that showed the Ethiopian masses marching forward, hammers and sickles raised as they tramped over the bodies of suit-coated Westerners. "Yankee go home," said smaller posters pasted all along the main boulevard. These black-and-white flyers showed an Ethiopian man strangling Uncle Sam.

The missionary who was driving clucked when he had to stop for a row of stones set across the street. Men stepped off the sidewalk carrying rifles, and approached the front window. They spoke to the white-haired driver with insolent scowls. They were wearing T-shirts and flip-flops. One had a New York Yankees cap on his head, and he walked the length of the van, looking in each window, passing his gaze over me as if I was a spare tire.

Another one of these neighborhood police, or *kebele*, demanded our passports. He flipped through them slowly, glancing at our faces. Then the man with the baseball cap decided that he wanted to open the back hatch, but the others argued with him and slapped the side of the van, waving us on.

This was definitely not the Ethiopia I had left six years earlier. I felt reminded instead of scenes from Orwell's *Nineteen Eighty-Four*, a book I had checked out from the Troy Library in preparation for our return. I could almost sense the surveillance and the inner caution it created. People walked with heads down, talking quietly. The only ones who met our eyes were soldiers, and their gaze revealed a smoldering disdain.

As I helped to carry our bags into the guesthouse at the mission headquarters, I became aware of the palpable stress that had built up in my body, but I also felt a buzz of energy that I had to admit, naive as I was, felt good. One measure of how in-the-moment I had become is that I had forgotten my mother entirely. I didn't think of her until the next day when Dad took Nat and me down to the cubicle at the guesthouse entrance to use the heavy rotary-dial phone.

After Nat had greeted Mom, I took a turn, and when she replied, her voice sounded as if she was speaking from inside a tunnel. My own voice echoed against itself, interrupting each new phrase. She said she was sitting in our stripped-down living room with no pictures on the walls and only one folding chair. Tomorrow she was going to move into Grandma's emptied bungalow so that renters could occupy our house.

"Grandma is finally on her feet," Mom said. "She began using a walker."

"That's great," I replied, hardly pausing before spilling out my own story about the bull-like porter at the London airport who had rejected our footlockers, saying, "Not today, Gov'nor. Those're big enough for coffins." I wanted to tell her what I'd seen in Addis, too, but I couldn't talk as openly. Dad had cautioned me not to say anything critical since the phone could be tapped.

"It's pretty interesting here," I added. "It's changed a lot."

"How?" she wanted to know, and I tried to think of a clever, coded way to explain about the huge billboards or the Soviet plane, but I couldn't shake the sense of some grim man in a room across the street with earphones on his head.

"You just need to see for yourself," I replied.

There was an odd pause, and I wondered if we had been cut off. "You there?" I asked, and when she said yes, I told her I'd better turn the phone over since a kid from the floor above our guest room had invited us to come shoot slingshots in the garden.

"He's the son of the mission director, Mr. Cumbers. You remember him, right?"

There was another pause, and I waited, sensing that something was troubling her.

"What's up?" I asked.

Mom sighed as if something had caught in her throat. "It just sounds like you're all doing so well . . . like you could get along fine whether I came or not. You sure you still need me?"

I felt as if I had been slapped. My mother had a disciplined ability to hold back her own feelings—to present only what was present-able. As a result, it had never occurred to me to think of her needing me—or needing me to need *her*. I was frightened by the very open-ness of her admission—made aware of how far away she really was and how mission life had always had this effect: separating us as a family. But I was also excited to go shoot slingshots in the garden, and to do it in a country where soldiers were patrolling the other side of the wall, cradling machine guns.

"No, Mom," I said, trying to quickly fix things. "It's not like that. Of course we need you. You've got to come right away. Have you talked to Dad about it?"

"It hasn't been easy, you know."

"Sorry, Mom. You gotta tell Dad. Here he is. Okay?"

It all seemed so dramatic—even my mother's distress on the other end of the telephone line. Back in Troy, what would my friends be do-ing on this day? Conjugating French verbs? Running the standard set of wind sprints in basketball practice? Would they flip the channel to *Happy Days*, singing "Rock Around the Clock"?

My new situation eclipsed such television entertainment because, after all, it was real. I was hyper-aware that I was really here and really in the middle of it all, no longer hearing about events as reported by Walter Cronkite on the *CBS Evening News*. At some level, I relished what the next day would bring because, whatever happened, it would be different.

Twelve

A few years ago, I was laughing my way through a set of old family photo albums (with the usual grainy and half-focused snapshots of family members hamming it up) when I came upon my parents' wedding album and flipped to this scripture verse inscribed on the first page: "For me to live is Christ, and to die is gain."

It was a shock to see this mutual pledge of allegiance—as if, to borrow a phrase from the Revolutionary War hero Patrick Henry, my parents had proclaimed at the wedding altar, "Give us Jesus or give us death." Yet I suppose I shouldn't have been stunned, given the way my parents had always lived, including the year 1977, when they took us into the middle of a communist battle zone.

The verse they chose for their marriage pledge is, as you may have guessed, a verse from one of the epistles of Paul, who was in jail at the time, awaiting possible execution. Unfazed, he boasted that he was ready to die, since dying would be "gain." It is this attitude that has made Paul the enduring poster boy of missionary recruitment—a sort of biblical super-Marine. As the first real missionary of the Christian church, he logged up fourteen thousand miles taking the Good News to the ends of the earth as he understood it, even though that meant shipwreck, whippings, stoning, repeated jailing, and eventual death. His efforts to reach unbelievers in places such as Tarsus, Corinth, Thessalonica, and Rome—building up a new Christian empire—pitted him directly against the military might of the Roman Empire, and he naturally turned to metaphoric battle terminology, urging, "Put on the breastplate of righteousness and take up the sword of the spirit."

Today, Paul remains the measure of fearless commitment, and I imagine that my parents, when they decided to take us into Ethiopia, were thrilled at the prospect of finally exercising their courage enough to enlist and to wade into the fray. Yes, my mother showed a moment of distress when she admitted on the phone her sense of abandonment, but her hesitation was not about wanting us to return from Ethiopia so much as wanting to board a plane and join us. What could be more meaningful really than to risk everything for Jesus? True, we would be running right into the fire, but what place was safer than there—in the very will of God?

My parents' attitude was not that different than the attitude of their exemplar, Dr. Lambie, who risked it all when he left the station he had so diligently built on a tributary of the Nile so that he could start over in the completely unknown territory of Ethiopia, taking his family into a savannah town notorious for malaria and sleeping sickness. Lambie crossed over the border not long after the catastrophic World War I defeat of the British at Gallipoli in Turkey, and he was deeply impressed with what he heard about the unflinching courage of the British troops, thousands of whom climbed out of trenches and charged the Turkish machine guns despite knowing they would be mown down like all the previous groups. In response to their stoic example, he wrote: "To see the gallant soldiers willing to die for king and country with an utter lack of self-pity is a great lesson for Christians and missionaries, who often . . . are too solicitous for their own health and well-being. Oh for a greater abandonment to God, enabling us to approach a zero hour with equanimity, to risk our lives with a dashing elañ for our God."

Put simply, this was the model of my youth: a kind of spiritual war ethic in keeping with the American Marine motto "Semper Fidelis"— "Always Faithful." I was being taught that life on the front lines— loyal to the end—was admirable, and though no one was saying it outright, I was also learning that perhaps life without such challenges was hardly worth living—which may be the reason I can feel so inexplicably empty some winter mornings here in Iowa, more than three decades later, as I step back into the house, New York Times in hand, and sit down to read about "real life" happening somewhere else across the globe.

I suppose that most military personnel feel similarly, and that may explain the way they struggle to return to "normal" life after war or why they tend to have a unique bond to a group of others who served alongside them—something that not even a spouse can understand or replace. I suppose it is why, sometimes, even though I do not condone war (being bothered that the opponents in a religious conflict are always equally convinced they have a corner on the truth), I can still feel quite dissatisfied in my comfortable house with my wife nearby, warming her feet at the fireplace, and with my sons in the next room, practicing happily at their drums and guitar.

Into the Furnace

My object in life is to dethrone God and destroy capitalism.

KARL MARX

He said, "Look! I see four men walking around in the fire, unbound and unharmed, and the fourth looks like a son of the gods."

DANIEL 3.25

Thirteen

A fter a weekend at the mission headquarters, Dad accompanied Nat and me to Bingham Academy, riding with us in the back of a VW van driven by an Ethiopian staff worker. Once we were on the streets—outside the mission compound with its stone wall and toothed ridge of broken bottles—I felt again the strangeness of being back in Ethiopia. Some of that sensation, no doubt, came from the change in climate. Only three days earlier I had been shivering in a parka outside our house, the dead lawn glistening with frost. As my father had gathered us together with church friends, the air seemed crisp in my nostrils, sanitized by the cold. Here, by contrast, each breeze carried its own amalgam of earthy scents: dust and donkey droppings, chili pepper and the wet slop of wash water, eucalyptus smoke and flowering frangipani.

As we drove along, swerving around craters in the asphalt, a river of pedestrians parted, pressing against the tin fences. They jumped aside even more quickly as an olive-green truck came honking down the other lane followed by a jeep with a soldier standing in the back, gripping the handles of a mounted machine gun. Afterward, though, they leaped right back over the ditches and took over the street: men in wool suit jackets quick-walking to the office, old women swaying under bundles of kindling, a pair of turbaned priests tapping along with walking sticks, and all of them so different than the neighbors I had known in Troy, Kansas, that I marveled at their very "otherness": light-brown skin with high cheekbones, as much Arab as African, as if Egyptians and Kenyans had been meeting here for a thousand years to marry and make their own race.

A roadside kiosk shot past, emblazoned with the bright red-and-white slogan of international capitalism: Coca-Cola®. Then came a series of "Go-Home-Yankee" posters, featuring a bug-eyed Uncle Sam being strangled.

Another half a mile and we had to stop, halted by kebele sentries who quizzed our driver on the purpose of his trip. Pedestrians sidled around us. If anyone looked into the van, they looked away quickly, as if not sure we should exist. I was not sure I should exist either, here in this very different world where I stuck out like a neon sign blinking "foreign, foreign, foreign." I tried to wear a vaguely apologetic smile, as if to say, "I know, it's crazy isn't it?" As we eased back into traffic, I looked up at the trees that lifted their tall limbs overhead: a fleecy jacaranda with its umbrella of purple blossoms, and the ridged pole of a royal palm bursting into a spray of spiked leaves.

When we drew closer to the school, I thought I recognized a lumberyard. Men in ragged pants were hoisting planks onto a Fiat truck—long, rough-hewn planks that hadn't been squared off. Their curly hair was flecked with sawdust.

Then came a familiar forest of young eucalyptus trees, tall and thin with silver-green leaves hanging down like spearheads. Through the screen of tree trunks I could see the chain-link fence of Bingham, sided with tin, and the cinderblock wall of the two-story dorm I had lived in as a seven- and eight-year-old. I turned toward Nat to say something, but he was staring out the window pensively, his eager grin gone. His thirteen-year-old face seemed pale and vulnerable under its bowl of sandy hair, which forced me to recall momentarily what I had felt the first time I was left at Bingham eight years earlier: how my brother Johnathan tried to console me, seeing that I was crying, and how he took me into his dorm, arm over my shoulder, then knelt down beside me and prayed for the Lord to protect me, to keep me from hurting so badly.

Swept by old emotions, I thought of Johnathan back in the United States by himself. He was the first to go to boarding school, without anyone to offer consolation. Now he was alone again. I couldn't do much for him, but I could at least try to help Nat. "Don't worry," I told him, "you're going to like it."

The driver honked and we eased through the main gate, greeted by the *zebunya*, a smiling guard who saluted and banged back one wing of the tin gates with a cudgel. Though six years had passed, the Academy looked almost exactly as it had before. A yellow tetherball hung from a pole. The gym was still an asphalt floor with a corrugated roof on poles. And I felt a familiar sweep of emotion looking across the soccer pitch toward the tallest eucalyptus tree, recognizing its graceful outline against the fleecy clouds. I had gazed at that tree over and over from my third-grade classroom, seeing the steel-winged kites glide to their perches then swoop away, shouldering the sunlight.

Nat was assigned to a dormitory attached to Gowan Hall, a sprawling building that included a conference room, a cafeteria, and four or five other dormitory wings. To my surprise, I was housed instead back in the dormitory I had known as a child. It had been converted into a senior high hostel so that teenagers could board at Bingham while commuting to Good Shepherd Academy, a separate mission school large enough to offer high school classes.

My roommate even turned out to be one of the guys who had been a roommate in third grade, the same Dave who had suckered me into a pillow fight then leapt into his bunk so that I was left standing alone, pillow dangling, when our dorm father turned on the lights, ready to administer a strapping. Dave laughed after I reminded him of that incident, tall and lean-faced, his hair down over his eyes so that he had to flick it back. He had spent his Christmas vacation in the arid Muslim region of Jigjiga, not far from the Somalia border, so he was burnt brown by the sun.

Across the hall from us, I also recognized another of my former roommates, who was neither tanned nor easygoing. Brad got up stiffly from his desk, where he had been sitting straight-backed reading a Bible, and he shook my hand very formally. Then a couple of others wandered into the room, introducing themselves. But the ones I most hoped to see didn't show up. Dan Coleman was living with his parents in a separate house on campus, and Mari Dye wasn't allowed in the male wing.

I didn't see Mari until later that evening when Dave took me to a lounge downstairs and began to describe how we would all take turns in the shared kitchen making sack lunches. There was a playful shriek followed by a clatter of footsteps. Then Mari came bounding down the circular stairs chased by a dark-haired, sharp-faced fellow I didn't recognize. He caught her around the waist and threw her onto a nearby couch, from where she let out another shriek.

I knew it was Mari from the photo I had kept on my bulletin board in Troy, noting the same dimpled grin, the full cheeks, and wavy black hair. As she lay there, face flushed, she realized there was a stranger in the room, which caused her to bounce upright. Suddenly recognizing me, she blurted out "Hi," then leapt right back up the steps followed by her confused pursuer.

Mari had never said anything in her letters about boys she might like. I had secretly hoped she would be waiting and available. However, that seemed unlikely now. After I climbed into bed that night, I finally ventured an off-hand question: "So who was the guy with Mari Dye?"

"Oh, that's Brake. He's a freshman."

That's as much as I learned before my thoughts were interrupted by a sharp pop in the distance, as if some part of the city had been uncorked.

A burst of automatic rifle fire rattled in response, and I asked Dave, "Do they do this every night?"

"Yeah, man. That's the norm. If you can't sleep, try counting shots."

"What's going on?"

"Just rebels doing their thing. Soldiers retaliating. There's a bunch of groups trying to get control."

I fought down my fear, seeing that my roommate was being nonchalant. Still, I couldn't sleep. How impossible, it seemed, to push those shots out of my mind, knowing that people were out there in the dark risking death for what they believed. Was some resistance fighter on the ground, breathing a last breath, all his bravado gone cold? Was a door about to get pounded down so that a kebele leader could be assassinated? And what about Christians? Were they the target of some of these attacks? Should I have a plan, such as a hiding place? Did this building have an attic?

"Hey, are they going after church people too?" I murmured toward Dave's dark silhouette, but he was already sleep. And though it seemed wrong for me not to pay attention, after a long while I drifted out of conscious thought. I finally let go of the disturbing attempt to brace myself and did what was natural. I slept.

Fourteen

O n Sundays at Bingham Academy, when I was only seven or eight, I used to join all my dorm mates in the same weekly ritual, donning identical black suits and pants, stiff as stovepipe. We put on black dress shoes and black clip-on bowties and filed out the ramp of our dorm, turning the corner of the dorm toward the set-apart chapel. As we waited there in a row, we could hear the rest of the grade-school students inside, trumpeting the muffled words of our traditional entrance hymn, "Onward Christian soldiers, marching as to war," and we added our tremulous sopranos as we passed through the doors, calling out, "with the cross of Jesus going on before."

The old wooden chapel was stiff and creaky and lit by a few monochrome stained-glass windows that set down blocks of yellow sepia light, as if we were worshiping in an antique daguerreotype. Rowland Bingham was our patron saint, so to speak, having come to Africa in the 1890s, determined to reach the interior with the gospel or die trying. And out the back window, mottled by tinted glass, we could see Gowan Hall, named for Bingham's first missionary companion, one of the men who actually *did* die trying to bring the gospel to the interior.

Still today, if I hear that old English hymn, written at the height of the British Empire and popularized by the Salvation Army, it pitches me into a dark funk, creating an undertow of sad helplessness that my soul is simply not strong enough to swim out of. "Onward Christian Soldiers" is, to be blunt, my most deplored hymn because, despite such a visceral desire to reject it, the lyrics wield a powerful grip over me, calling me to come back to terms with what feels like an old weakness, a reluctance to do what is my duty, what I used to feel so powerless to accomplish at the early age of seven or eight.

That hymn raises a latent rebellion inside my older adult self, who wants to shout back: "No! This cannot be Jesus's way. He had no army at his back. He refused to lead a political movement. The only time someone unsheathed a sword on his behalf—when Peter struck off the ear of the High Priest's servant—Jesus told him to put the weapon away." However, I cannot escape the hard fact that on the night when he was betrayed by Judas, Jesus modeled a bold willingness to die, asking it of his followers as well. "Take up your cross," he said, "and follow me."

So there it is: the cross as a central rallying point, a battle standard lifted before the troops. And because of that, I am forced to ponder a kind of latent death-call that remains an unsettling core reality for committed Christians. It is all the more disturbing since now I am a middle-aged man conscious of my looming mortality. Does any social cause warrant such self-sacrifice? Theoretically, yes. Some things are simply more important than me. In fact, there might be relief in yielding to that reality. However, would I actually be willing to die if forced to decide? Is anything really that important to me? Workers' rights? Liberty? My children? God?

Fifteen

When I woke after that first night back in the Bingham dormitory, the distant crackle of gunfire had been replaced by normal sounds: trucks farting as they shifted gears, a car horn, a donkey braying. It was time for my first day of classes.

After breakfast at the Bingham cafeteria, where we were scrutinized by the stuffed, un-blinking heads of a greater kudu and several Thomson's gazelles, I followed the other high school students out of the cafeteria and climbed aboard the bus that would deliver us to Good Shepherd Academy. I was delighted to recognize Dan Coleman running to meet us. He was still sporting a shaggy mop of blonde hair and a strip of freckles across his nose. He grinned familiarly. Then he swung into the seat across the aisle from Dave Iwan and me.

"So you made it," he said with a wry twang, and I felt the odd sense that six years had just collapsed.

"I did," I replied, "and they put me back in the same dorm with Iwan. Total déjà vu."

"Recognize any of the old stuff? HQ? The Mercato? The red-light district?" I nodded, though I had been too young before to even realize what all those red bulbs represented.

He grinned back and called out commentary as we rolled onto the streets of Addis. For instance, when we passed a burnt-out hulk of a car, he said, "That's from before Christmas break. Some guerrilla dudes raided an army post and got a bunch of weapons, but they got trapped here."

"It was totally gross," Dave added from my other side. "You could see bodies for a week."

"Check out the bullet holes," Dan said. Then he frowned in a cockeyed way that suggested this was all so absurd you just had to find humor in it and keep moving. He still had his old enthusiasm, but he seemed less naive than when we were eight—back when he would suggest, hey, let's try to swing all the way round the crossbar on the swing set. He gazed over his shoulder at the receding car, tires burnt away, and shook his head before asking, "So, man, what's new in Kansas?"

What to say? This was all so jarringly different than the life I had just left that it was hard to find words. The only dangerous aspect of living in Troy was my own lack of judgment—like the day before Christmas break, when I had gotten my driving permit and made the mistake of racing around an icy bend, trying to pass my neighbor, only to feel the car swerve into a long, agonizing slide.

"Well, there aren't a whole lot of bodies lying around, except during a football game. I mean, this rebel stuff is nuts. Who were the guys who raided the army post?"

Dan looked to the driver of the bus, a twenty-five-year-old Ethiopian who seemed to be a favorite with all the teens. "Hey, Yared," Dan shouted. "What do you think about the burned-out car? Were those guys from the EDU?"

This driver, a slender guy with rippling forearms and a receding hairline, shook his head. "EPRP," he shouted.

"How do you know?"

"Because God told me."

Dan laughed, and I asked, "So what's the EPRP?"

"The Ethiopian People's Revolutionary Party," Dave explained. "They're the student radicals who started the whole thing. They say they want democracy, but they're more communist than Mengistu."

"And what's the other group?"

Dan jumped back in, "The Ethiopian Democratic Union. They're the ones who want to go back to an emperor. They're mainly Amharas, up in the north."

"And then there's the Eritrean Liberation Front," said Dave. "Don't forget them. And the Tigray People's Liberation Front."

After several stops at kebele checkpoints, we finally jolted off of the asphalt onto a rock-strewn road, and Dan leaned over to tell me we were nearing Good Shepherd. I noticed that people on each side of the road were living in crude shacks with cracked adobe walls. I looked more closely and saw that many of them were disfigured, with flattened noses and pocked faces. Dan explained that they were lepers from a nearby leprosarium, the same leprosarium begun by our mission founder, Dr. Lambie, when the emperor granted him permission to stay and work in Ethiopia.

The farther we went, the busier this road became. Kids dashed in front of the jolting bus to rescue a soccer ball made of bound plastic. A small herd of goats had to be whipped aside by teenage boys who gave us the evil eye. Women stared indifferently, looking up from open cooking fires where they squatted as they roasted grain or poured batter onto wide clay skillets.

This entire neighborhood was a beehive of activity, full of shouting children and dashing chickens and donkeys transporting bundles of firewood, and I felt acutely aware that I was an intruder, neither Ethiopian nor poor nor leprous. A turbaned priest, peeing against a mud wall, glanced over his shoulder, his eyes locking on mine. His face was gaunt, cheeks sunken where they disappeared under a shaggy beard. His gaze seemed full of stolid disapproval, and that made me more conscious of the separation between me and him, symbolized by the bus itself, which might as well have been a submarine passing through the depths.

After he zipped his trousers to turn away, a woman bowed low, lifting the gauzy *netta* from her head. She stayed bowed so that he could extend the tip of his walking stick, topped by a carved cross, which she kissed three times. Then I lost sight of this pair as we braked for a pothole and two boys raced to reach the slowing bus. The winner leaped right onto the bumper and stuck out his tongue. A moment later and he was gone, disappearing into the billowing dust as the bus rocked through the school gates.

When I stepped down for the first time onto the grounds of Good Shepherd Academy, I got the sensation that I was standing in an oasis of sorts—transported to a geographical parenthesis. The recent bustle of the road was screened by a high hedge, and the space on this side of the barrier stretched out in an uncluttered, park-like way. Just a few isolated buildings were scattered across a tree-lined lawn, and only a few kids could be seen strolling out of what seemed to be a dining hall. They were all Anglos except for some company and diplomat kids from African countries, and even those kids were wearing standard Western garb: blue jeans and T-shirts with slogans like "Keep on trucking."

I didn't have long to consider the scene, though. "C'mon," Dave urged, and he pointed to a building around a big bank of shrubs. "We've got Bible class first."

Sixteen

As a child flying on Ethiopian Airlines, I used to love studying the laminated brochure in my seat pocket, which featured a dozen painted panels like a cartoon strip, depicting the Queen of Sheba traveling to Israel to meet King Solomon, then having a son from their union who, according to legend, brought the Ark of the Covenant home with him, the first of many kings who claimed the title "Lion of Judah."

These little paintings were distinctively Ethiopian—with a traditional palette of green, red, and yellow and with robed characters who stared out at the viewer from luminous almond-shaped eyes. If eyes were windows to the soul, then these large-eyed people were amazingly soulful. Even as a six- or seven-year-old, I viewed them with reverent awe. In my mind Sheba and Menelik were not just royalty but saints.

Actually, I also regarded Emperor Hailie Selassie (whose name meant "Holy Trinity") in a similar manner, awed by his ancestral tie to biblical royalty. As a grade-school kid, I was convinced of his claim to be yet another Lion of Judah. In that sense, I was not so different than Jamaican Rastafarians who had latched onto the emperor's earlier title, *Ras Tafari* (or "He who inspires awe").

What I didn't realize as that wide-eyed child in the 1960s was that for over 1,500 years, the Orthodox church had been bolstering the Ethiopian High King. Church leaders could see that without the emperor, the power of the church would be gone, so they were quite careful to reinforce his near-divine mystique.

Ever since the converted Crown Prince Ezana ascended the throne and instituted Christianity as a state religion in the fourth century AD (even requiring baptism for his appointed officials), the Orthodox church had maintained such a strong influence over the royal court that it amassed great wealth, similar to the Roman church of medieval Europe. The Orthodox patriarch and his priests owned large tracts of land and exercised an even wider oversight, since practically all regions were owned and managed by the ruling Amharas and their church-sanctioned aristocracy.

This "appointed-by-God" ruling class was particularly heavy-handed in regions south of Addis Ababa, where the Amharas treated other tribal groups as sharecropping serfs or slaves, conducting slave raids right up until World War II. In fact, when Dr. Lambie was permitted by Hailie Selassie to begin the first mission station at Soddo, traveling three weeks south by mules to where my parents would eventually be stationed along with the Barlows, he had to care for several patients who were shot by Amhara slavers.

Is it any wonder, as a result, that when these disenfranchised tenant farmers—forced to pay as much as half of their harvest as tax—began to carry placards and go to the streets shouting, "Land to the tiller," they were at odds with not only the emperor and his Amhara landlords but the church that had buttressed the system? Is it any wonder that one of the first major leaders to be deposed was the head patriarch, Abune Tewflos?

It used to seem so odd to me—as a teen looking at the huge billboard of Marx, Engels, and Lenin at Red Square—that Russian communism would have such widespread appeal in Ethiopia. I knew that we, as American Protestants, were foreigners with a foreign ideology, but what made the cadres of USSR any less foreign or suspect? Why were all these Russian consultants being flown in from snowbound Moscow, and Ethiopian politicians taking emptied seats right back into that dour land?

The emerging affinity didn't make sense to me until decades later when I began to think about historical parallels such as the emperor-like Tsar who had been supported by the Russian Orthodox church, or a land-holding Russian aristocracy that had claimed divine authority. In Russia, after the overthrow of the Tsar, one of the first actions of the new government was to appoint their own head of the Orthodox church, then to remove the royal chair—or throne—from the cathedral of Moscow, where Peter the Great had been coroneted in 1682. For the empire to end, the church's influence must end. Soon, no citizen could claim membership in the church and be a member of the Communist Party. No church member could expect to get a university education or a promotion or a political appointment.

I didn't know any of that as an awestruck six-year-old with an in-flight brochure painted in the manner of traditional icons. I just knew that the art was beautifully mysterious. And though I sensed from my parents that, for some reason, the Orthodox priests were not to be trusted, I had no idea how much tension actually existed between "their people" and "ours." My parents, I suspect, did not want to alarm me with reports of priests stoning mission converts who tried to distribute gospel tracts—or of Orthodox believers digging up the corpses of buried evangelicals and tossing them out of the cemeteries. They didn't want me to worry about the arrests that were happening right up until the revolution, caused by priests who felt that the upstart Protestants were undermining the proper order of the culture, showing complete disregard for the ancient hierarchy that put men over women and elders over youth, not to mention landed gentry over working class.

When, finally, Emperor Selassie was overthrown, the Orthodox church took it on the chin, but the much smaller mission-related churches received a double blow. Now they were distrusted not only by the Orthodox leaders (who still exercised a degree of control), but also by the Marxists, who looked to the mission churches as a convenient scapegoat. Such Protestants were more suspect than Orthodox believers because they were so clearly associated with the Soviet Union's most despised enemies—capitalist countries like England and Canada and, worst of all, the United States of America.

Seventeen

Upon entering my first classroom at Good Shepherd Academy that January of 1977, I felt forced into the spotlight. When Dan and Dave introduced me to our Bible teacher, a thickset, hairy man with a wrestler's grip, he shouted out, "This is our newest student, class. Everyone say, 'Hello, Tim.'"

"Hello Tim," they echoed, and a few waved good-naturedly, as if expecting me.

Then without any further fanfare, the teacher pointed me to a desk and leaped into his summary of the semester. He wanted us to understand that we would be concentrating on major and minor prophets, having already covered the creation account and Exodus. To begin with, we would look at the prophet Elijah in the Book of Kings, who confronted wicked King Ahab and his pagan wife Jezebel less than eighty years after Makeda, the Queen of Sheba, made her vaunted visit to Solomon's court.

Mr. Brown passed out Bibles as he covered the syllabus. Then he had us take turns reading aloud. We read about how Elijah came out of his hiding place, a cave in the desert, to confront the false prophets Jezebel had brought into Israel. We read how Elijah set up a religious duel on the peak of Mount Carmel, where he and the priests of Baal built altars and slaughtered bulls, putting the cut meat on stacks of wood. Then how the pagan priests slashed themselves as they begged for their god to send down fire and consume the offering.

"Shout louder," Elijah taunted. "Maybe he is sleeping."

When it was his own turn, by contrast, Elijah commanded that pots of water be poured over the wood and meat, after which he made a single, simple prayer: "O LORD, God of Abraham, Isaac and Israel, let it be known today that you are God in Israel and that I am your servant. . . ."

Voilà! Fire shot down from heaven, intense enough to incinerate even the rocks under the offering. The people of Israel were so impressed that they chased the priests of Baal into a valley and slaughtered them all.

What a change from U.S. history at Troy High School! How loaded these passages seemed, echoing off the backdrop of communist Ethiopia. For me, they brought to mind Ethiopians like Elijah, who were hiding from their own tyrannical ruler, perhaps hoping for fire from heaven! Yet what to do with the bloodlust at the end of the passage, and the 450 corpses stacked in a pile? What to do with Mr. Brown, too, who taught the whole story as if it was utterly removed—an archeological fragment engraved in ancient foreign letters?

I wasn't really sure what to think because Mr. Brown seemed oddly out of sync with the world around him. Unlike anyone else—student or faculty—he wore carefully pressed khaki shorts, and his shirt was buttoned to the top, tight around his Adam's apple. When he took a turn reading from the Book of Kings, he shouted as if we were deaf, putting an eccentric spin on the word "Israel" so that the first syllable got its own elongated fanfare—"ISSS-rye-el."

I checked to see if I was the only one to find his manner weird, and I noticed Dave was smirking. Dan lifted an eyebrow, too, as if to say, "Aren't we having fun now?"

So my day began, and as I made my way to the next class and the next, I was encouraged to see that students were friendly and most teachers less eccentric than Mr. Brown. My English class seemed especially promising. The teacher there—"Ali Jo" as Dan and Dave called her when she was out of earshot—was an inventive person who was going to let us write parodies of Shakespeare. To start the semester, though, she wanted us to read from a journal kept by Aleksandr Solzhenitsyn, a Russian Christian who had been targeted by Stalin's secret police and sent to a Siberian prison camp to labor alongside other dissidents.

Unlike Mr. Brown, Ali Jo was clear that we might find parallels between this reading and our own lives. She said we had to write journal entries in response. And so that afternoon, after Yared drove us back to Bingham, I carried the first set of mimeographed pages into the trees behind the dormitory to sit and read.

The ink from the duplicator gave off an alcoholic tang as I dipped into a tale about a log Solzhenitsyn threw onto the fire when he was a prisoner in Siberia. Ants dashed out of the burning log, zigzagging in panic. Some fell away, singed. They dropped with little hisses into the flames until Solzhenitsyn removed the log from the blaze, compelled by sympathy.

For a while I sat there musing, distracted only after some curious grade-school boys came by and asked who I was, having never seen me on campus. Once they drifted away, I had to get my mind back on track. What could I write in response to Solzhenitsyn's log full of ants?

I balked at leaving a written record, something that could be used to throw me in prison like Solzhenitsyn, whose only "crime" had been writing a letter that included a critical comment about Stalin. At first, I made a safe biblical comparison, linking the burning ants to the story of Shadrach, Meshach, and Abednego, three Israelites who were thrown into a huge furnace when they wouldn't bow to the conquering king Nebuchadnezzar. True, the three persecuted men had been visited by an angel and had stood unscathed in the flames, but I wondered about other resisters who might have been sentenced to the flames with no rescuing angel, and that brought me back to Christians here in contemporary Ethiopia. Weren't they also getting "burned" by their government? After all, like Elijah or Shadrach and his friends, they too had refused to bow to the godlike authority of a despot.

Emboldened, I left the biblical comparisons and started to write about my father's friend Sahle Tilahun, although I altered his name to protect his identity. Sahle had told my father, after welcoming us at the Headquarters' dining hall, that communist leaders were now forcing all teachers to go to reeducation camps. He and his wife, both teachers, had been forced to attend week-long indoctrinations far to the west of Addis, where every day they were schooled in Marxist philosophy. When tested, they dared not disagree. Since each question tended to be a question of fact—Who introduced a materialist philosophy that critiqued idealistic philosophies?—they felt they could write the correct answer—Marx—without compromising their beliefs. Who criticized Hegel's philosophy as a kind of spiritual idealism? Marx again. Or who said that material life as we know it began due to a combination of necessity and chance? Darwin.

Such answers were no problem for them. "My wife got them all correct," Sahle said, grinning slyly. However, in the evenings all the camp attendants were required to stand at attention and shout revolutionary slogans: "Down with imperialism! Down with capitalism! Down with America!" Over and over, they were told to shout, "Long live Marxism!"

Sahle and Aberash couldn't, in good conscience, make such a proclamation. Proclaiming allegiance to Marxism felt like a betrayal of their real faith; only God would live forever. And in Aberash's case, the commander of the camp noticed that she was not joining the chorus. The scornful woman confronted her, shouting in front of all the teachers: "Why are you not cooperating? Are you an idealist?"

"I believe in Jesus," said Aberash, "since his philosophy comes from God."

"There is no god, you fool. And you are an enemy because you are blocking our progress. You are standing in the way of the workers."

She pointed at Aberash and screamed to all the assembled teachers, "This is our enemy. Down with her. Down with all idealists. Say it with me. . . ."

As I wrote, I sat so still that an ant climbed out of the grass onto my pants and scurried onto my shirt, its filament antennae probing. When it ventured onto my arm and paused on that fleshy bridge with its hair-like legs tickling my skin, I felt an urge to brush it away, but I stayed completely motionless, marveling that such a tiny creature could be two things at once, both a literal insect with a red-beaded body and a symbol for something larger. Ant as more than ant. Fire as more than fire. Log as more than log.

In the Ethiopian prison camps, just as in the Siberian camps, Christians were now getting thrown into the furnace of Marxism. We had already heard reports that in the prison where Dr. Barlow's trainee Waja had been incarcerated, jailers were trying to demoralize Christians by tearing up Bibles and tossing them in the latrine as toilet paper. Instead, the prisoners were keeping single pages and passing them around, memorizing them so that they would not be lost. They were creating a kind of shared internal Bible that could not be taken away.

One of the men who had joined this secret confederation, ironically, was the very man who had betrayed Waja to the kebele near Bulki, causing his pharmacy to be ransacked. Now a detainee, he had shown up in the prison yard hobbling due to infected shackle sores, and because the guards trusted Waja as their ad hoc physician, they had let him treat the injured man. Instead of shunning his enemy, Waja had helped to heal him.

Such fierce kindness was inspiring. In my own small way, I wanted to stand in solidarity, at least to support my parents in their support of such people. Naturally, I was afraid that some kebele sentry might open my notebook and be able to read in English. I was afraid, too, that I might be forced to deny my own faith or be carted away. But when I thought of people like Waja and Sahle and Aberash, people like Solzhenitsyn or Elijah, I knew I had to be braver than this. I had to be brave enough to at least write down these thoughts. I might not be ready to speak my mind on the street, but I could start on paper.

Eighteen

ack when I was only fifteen and we flew into Addis, it was exciting to feel like we were joining a secret maneuver meant to bring support to allies—a little like characters in one of those black-and-white World War II movies made by Hollywood patriots. It was romantic to think of myself as a military agent parachuting into occupied France, hoping to bolster the Resistance. At the time there was no irony for me about this engage-the-enemy mindset. Although Jesus had not used many military comparisons, Paul, the doctrinal strategist of the emerging church, had said that we, as Christians, would be confronted by principalities and powers and that we needed to be prepared, even ready to take the offensive. Though Paul did not model a physical battle, he called for spiritual warfare—a willingness to stand up for what we believed, unashamed of God.

As soon as we were greeted by the missionaries in Addis, I could sense the same dramatic determination. They were, in essence, conducting a revolution within the revolution, and that was more rousing than standard missionary work. It gave every decision a new level of Purposefulness, a kind of Determined Intent that I felt as soon as we ate our first dinner at "Headquarters," a term that (by the way) has its own warlike connotations.

Before the food was served, we bowed in prayer, and the missionary at the head of the table brought up a list of staff and Ethiopian ministers around the country, asking God to protect each of them and to give them strength. Ato Sahle was there, too, telling us about the indoctrination camps and about secret "coffee clubs" of Christians who met at night in homes. And during the meal, I saw an intense animation in the faces of the veterans as they described to Dad (their newly arrived reinforcement) the remarkable church growth that was taking place even though buildings were being nailed shut or ministers arrested.

Together, the missionaries and local Christians were making subversive plans that would keep a hidden resistance movement alive, even scheming how to recruit new members. Dad wanted to hear it all, so Nat and I finally left him there with Sahle and two fellow missionaries to go to our room upstairs. We were "bit players" stepping off stage, and as I looked back from the door, their close, absorbed conversation had the appearance of a filmed battle preparation—as if they were costumed actors hunkered down in a bunker with maps laid out. They might as well have been shifting brass icons that represented troop movements, lines of defense, key targets, support routes, and (only if absolutely necessary) corridors of retreat.

What many people may not realize, if they have not had much interaction with the evangelical Protestant church, is just how aggressive members can become when considering the wider world. Evangelicals feel obliged to spread their beliefs around the globe in obedience to a heavenly king: that is, Jesus. This campaign is not just about clergy either. People in the pews are committed to reaching every country and group of people, a goal that solidified over the last two centuries in response to a pivotal passage at the end of the Gospel of Matthew: "Therefore go and make disciples of all nations, . . . teaching them to obey everything I have commanded you."

Just a bit of related history: In 1910, when Dr. Lambie was establishing a station on the Sobat River in Sudan, quite close to the border of Ethiopia, another well-traveled missionary named Charles T. Studd came to Africa, having worked in China and India. He was a charismatic former athlete, known internationally for his exploits on the national cricket team of England, and he began a mission in the Belgian Congo called Heart of Africa Mission, which expanded quickly under the capable administration of his wife back in England (who, by the way, went a full twelve years at one point without seeing her husband).

Africa was not enough for the Studds, so they eventually renamed their mission "World Evangelization Crusade" and began sending missionaries to South America, Central Asia, and the Middle East. And by 1964, one of the members of this aptly named "Crusade" had put together a guidebook that is still in print, having been revised every five or ten years to give key evangelistic statistics on every country in the world. Like any large battle plan, this book has its own dynamic title, the equivalent of "Operation Desert Storm" or "Operation Rolling Thunder." It is labeled *Operation World*, and it serves as the main catalyst and resource for today's American evangelicals.

Inside *Operation World*, every current nation is described, with a political map, a list of ethnic groups, different languages, customs, and predominant religions. Most importantly, *Operation World* identifies the remaining people groups who may have had no exposure to Christianity—groups labeled as "Unreached." These are the ones with a kind of electric buzz around them, thrilling to any missionary-minded evangelical because they are the biggest challenge. If Jesus described his followers as fisher of men, then these unreached people are the monster fish—most difficult and satisfying to catch.

Reaching one of the unreached is not for the timid since they tend to live in remote areas hostile to foreign influence. It requires the sort of risk-taking bravado modeled by Charles T. Studd, who asserted, "Some want to live within sound of church or chapel bell; I want to run a rescue shop within a yard of hell."

Today, missionaries who risk going into unreached areas are not necessarily trying to conquer political territory, as in the Crusades of the medieval period. They hope to establish a spiritual kingdom instead, transcending earthly boundaries by bringing people through the gates of heaven. This mission lends them a deeply meaningful sense of purpose. The only problem is that it can also become an excuse for imposing cultural values or, even worse, elevating the self. All of us, at some deep level, want to be personally significant, and one of the great risks of going into another country with a rescuer's mentality is that it can lead to egotism—a generous, well-meaning, very humble sort of hubris that is, nonetheless, hubris.

Nineteen

uring the first few weeks of classes, my brother Nat seemed to be getting along well, although I didn't know for sure since I was at Good Shepherd on most weekdays. We were able to check in only occasionally, like the Sunday evening when I found him seated on our bus with a group of junior high students who had decided to come to an evening service at mission headquarters—one of the few Western-style services the government allowed, since it was in English and inside a foreign compound.

I high-fived Nat as I came down the aisle, getting a salute from his new friend Paul, the same boy who had taken us around the garden of the Headquarters shooting slingshots when we arrived in Ethiopia.

"How goes it?" I asked, and Nat lifted both thumbs.

"I thought grade school and junior high already had church."

"Yeah, but they said older kids could go with you guys. It's our only way out, you know."

I hadn't thought about the fact that Nat had not left the Bingham compound since we arrived. I felt sorry for him, as I had been across Addis twenty times or more. I wanted to sit down and talk, feeling strange about how little we had actually seen each other or talked. However, all seats were taken, so I was forced to move on down the aisle to where Mari Dye was sitting. Screwing up my courage, I asked, "Mind if I join you?"

I plopped down beside her, but she looked panicked and blurted out, "Actually, I'm saving that place for Donnie." So I stood up again, this time shuffling all the way to the last bench.

While we jolted down the pocked streets, seeing the last bit of sun slip away behind the western mountains, I stared fiercely through the rear window, feeling cut off. I tried not to give attention to Mari or her now-confirmed boyfriend, who had swung blithely into the seat I vacated. Instead, I glared at the scenes that unfolded behind the bus. Two men greeted each other with a traditional embrace, cheek to cheek; then they adjusted the *shammas* on their shoulders. A haughty woman stared straight ahead in a blue dented cab, her light-brown forehead glistening where her hair had been pulled back in a woven coiffure. A military jeep pulled onto the road behind us, taking the space where the taxi used to be.

It was early February, and we had just heard that seven leaders from the shadowy Derg—the Committee of Equals—were executed, condemned as counterrevolutionaries in the state newspaper. Mengistu was making it clear once again that he was the supreme commander and no one should think of challenging him. Rumor had it that he had even brought his personal bodyguards into the main committee meeting, right there at the Palace of Menelik, then pointed out the seven perceived enemies and followed them into the basement to help with the execution.

The city was on high alert, stationing more soldiers on the streets than ever. Here was another patrolling jeep, which should have made me extra cautious; however, I was too upset by Mari's rejection to really think. I stared at the soldier who was standing in the rear of the vehicle clamping the handles of the swiveling machine gun. He was not much older than me. I noticed the dirt on the lenses of his goggles and the bulging red cloth he had tied over his hair. I decided he looked foolish with his bug-like eyes and the barrel of his gun poking forward like the proboscis of an insect.

I kept staring at him with no thought for how my gaze might be interpreted—until the driver of the jeep suddenly pointed at me and shouted over his shoulder. Then the gun barrel came up, aimed at my chest, and with a snarl the gunner began to jerk as if riding a jackhammer.

I fell to the floor, heart hammering. When I peered down at my torso, I expected a row of bloody holes, so I was confused to find myself intact. Was I hallucinating?

Still terrified, I dared to peek back through the little window at the bottom of the rear door, and I saw the goggled gunner slapping at the helmet of the driver, grinning wildly. His teeth were bright white. He swung the gun toward me again and vibrated, roaring at his own joke.

This time, since my adrenaline had worn off, I nearly fainted. The strange thing is that still no one had noticed what was happening, as they were closer to the front and faced forward. When I climbed back onto the rear seat of the bus, I felt more alone than ever, hunched over with my undisclosed terror.

I fixed my eyes on the floor, clammy and nauseated. I was still in that state when we arrived at the mission headquarters. As I got off the bus with dusk settling over the city, it seemed as if I had come unmoored from my body, like a helium balloon rising over my head. Although my classmates were right in front of me, goofing around while they filed into the chapel, I felt completely removed. I didn't realize until ten minutes into the service, after we had sung an open-ing hymn and heard a prayer, that my father was actually going to be the guest speaker.

The usual minister, a choleric red-faced man with a shock of sil-ver hair, explained that Dr. Bascom had just returned from a special medical mission in southern Ethiopia, so we would hear from him rather than receiving a homily. Apparently, Dad had taken several days to travel south, far past our old stations at Leimo and Soddo, eventually reaching the dusty savannah town of Arba Minch along-side a lake in the Rift Valley. He had gone to offer a mobile clinic, which meant taking a visiting lady doctor with him, plus a translator. As it turned out, he had asked our old friend, Sahle Tilahun, to be the translator, since Sahle had lost his job as a school principal after being jailed briefly for spreading "subversive ideas"—in essence, handing out gospel tracts.

Sahle had come to this service along with Dad—to help with the "sermon"—so he joined my father at the pulpit. With his soft shy smile, he seemed the antithesis of someone who might be picked out by communist cadres as a threat. Maybe it was because he refused to take anything too seriously. He seemed to see humor everywhere, laughing at any absurdity, whether the cruel twists of fate brought on by the revolution or the zany high jinks of my father when a fan belt broke on their Land Rover.

"Sahle was not translating well for a while," Dad explained while patting Sahle on the shoulder, "because he wouldn't stop laughing as I made a substitute fan belt out of Dr. Dina's leather belt and a roll of duct tape. And when that broke, which forced me to improvise with shoestrings, we thought we were going to have to give him CPR."

Quickly assuming his role as the straight man, Sahle broke in: "Well, to be honest, it was very much dangerous to my health, I think. Traveling with this man, I might say, can be more dangerous than any kebele checkpoint."

People actually clapped, released for a moment from all the worries of the outside world. A joke! Even better, a joke about checkpoints!

So the two men went on with their unorthodox approach, making so many comic asides that before long the whole church was rollicking right back to the rows where the senior high usually kept their sleepy silence.

Dad explained that when his little medical team was still far from Addis, out in the sandy acacia forest, the shoestring fan belt snapped, so they had to stop in the shade next to a giant anthill and try to come up with a new option. While waiting, Sahle fell into conversation with a cluster of people who had stepped out of the bushes. All the women had long sticks tied to their grass skirts, and when Dad asked about the sticks, Sahle explained that these left trails in the dirt so that each man could find his wife.

"Go ahead. Tell them how the men knew which trail went with which woman."

"Ahbeit," said Sahle, looking sternly at my father. "I do not think they will let us back in this church. . . ."

"No, it's fine. I'm sure."

"All right then. The stick was moving just with the woman's body. Like this," he added, and he stepped from behind the pulpit to sway his hips.

The students loved this stuff. Here was a sermon like none they had heard before: broken fan belts and hip-waggling trails. The whole section around me began laughing.

Next, my father, who was never one to waste an opportunity for evangelism, explained how he and Sahle had found a biblical parallel for this stick-in-the-dust accessory, telling the gathered crowd that each person left a trail that was distinct and only God knew these trails, which meant God could come and find us if we got lost.

"It's true," Sahle added, letting his shy smile peek through. "I can say for sure, God knows just the way we walk."

Apparently, the only repair option that was left, out there in the acacia forest, was to replace the broken fan belt with the visiting doctor's pantyhose, which she graciously offered. To their amazement, the hose lasted another half an hour. "I'm assuming it was due to prayer," Dad said, "because there was a lot of prayer around those pantyhose—probably more prayer than any pantyhose has ever gotten."

In any case, when they finally neared the checkpoint close to Shashemane station, with the substitute belt shredded and the brakes going soft, my father had to bring the vehicle down into third gear and second, grinding finally into first, so that he would not roll past the point where a sentry was manning a gun.

Sahle jumped out to put a rock behind the wheel, which caused all the other sentries to swing their rifles off their straps. They were not amused. And after one of them discovered a bundle of Amharic gospel tracts in the trunk, their lieutenant shook the pamphlets in the air, snarling, "This is poison. The drug of America. Don't you know? There is no God."

Instead of staying silent, my father blurted out: "So how did all of this come into being—that thornbush, that bird, you and me?"

"It was not God."

"So it just happened?"

"It was not God."

"Can you believe it?" Sahle interjected. "Uncle Charley—that's what I call him—just threw down a tool from the back of the car, and he asked that soldier, 'How did it get there? Did it decide for itself?'"

The listeners at the chapel in Addis smiled warmly, seeing how Dad was challenging the Marxist notion of chance origins behind the universe.

Sahle was on a roll as he continued, "It was beautiful, I am telling you. Just the way he asked them to explain, 'How did the tool get there?' I could see they did not know what to say. Their dialectical materialism is good only for the classroom. It does not explain who made the tool or who moved it. It does not explain how the world began."

I was still in shock somewhat from the near-death experience on the bus, but I was heartened by the bold way my father and Sahle were talking up there at the front of the church. I was warmed, too, by their amused smiles. I wanted to be as brave. God called for courage, assuring us that he had counted the hairs on our heads—that he even knew when a sparrow fell. Surely, then, God had seen what took place on the bus earlier—had been there watching, ready to intervene if necessary.

Although I hardly got a chance to hug my father after the service, on the way back to the Academy in the dark, I relished the admiring comments that came from his unconventional "sermon." This time I was sitting with Nat and his friend Paul, feeling more like a part of the group.

"Cool sermon," Paul said. And Dan Coleman chipped in from a seat behind me, "Man, your dad is a total weed," which I took to be positive.

I grinned, conscious that it was now past 8:30 p.m. and quite dark —conscious, too, that if we were not back through the Bingham gate within an hour, we would be out illegally. For a moment, I could see the bug-eyed soldier with a red bandana, snarling as he swung the mounted gun toward me. Being out after curfew was no joke, I thought. But if it had to happen for some reason, we would be okay. I must trust. After all, the same God that my father had defended from the pulpit was the creator of the universe, the one with the master plan. This God was in charge of all the laws of nature, so that a pair of pliers would clank down properly if tossed into the air and the moon would swoop around the earth in a faithful circle. With such strength on my side, surely I had nothing to fear.

Twenty

The Marxist critique of Christian evangelism is not the sort of thing most children contemplate. By high school, students might start to entertain such ideas if their culture is ripe for revolt; however, I was a slow learner. It took me until graduate school—after I had stepped outside my circle of origin—to see the mission culture in a new light, and that was only because I began studying under a fleet of literary scholars who had tuned into Marxist theory due to the upheavals of the Vietnam War and the civil rights movement.

As part of my graduate studies, I read Chinua Achebe's Nigerian masterpiece *Things Fall Apart*, and I remember feeling stunned by the rich way of life that existed in the Igbo clan prior to the entry of colonial Christianity. Interviewed about his writing, Achebe stated that, if nothing else, he hoped it would show his own people that "their past—with all its imperfections—was not one long night of savagery from which the first Europeans acting on god's behalf, delivered them." Certainly that was the effect it had on me, even as an Anglo-American reader. Here was a pre-European way of life so remarkably vibrant that I could only grieve when the power of the clan was broken and Okonkwo, champion of the old ways, went off to hang himself from a tree. Despite the destructive hubris Okonkwo had shown, he was representative of a culture so fascinating that I could only grieve when the rigid missionary named Reverend Smith stood back gloating, supported by a group of converts who had emerged from the malcontents on the fringe of Igbo society.

I grieved and, in a troubling new way, I felt embarrassed. Had my parents, as missionaries, caused similar losses? Had I myself?

In Achebe's novel the missionary Reverend Smith works closely with a colonial administrator from England who is quite proud about a manuscript he has been creating, *The Pacification of the Primitive Tribes of the Lower Niger.* Politician and minister cooperate in breaking down the traditional structure of the Igbo society. And ironically, the death of the last great hero in this clan is hardly given a footnote in the district commissioner's manuscript, suggesting just how little these invading British understood the rich culture doomed with Okonkwo's demise.

For the district commissioner and for the bull-headed Reverend Smith, being Christian is being civilized and being civilized is being Christian. They are warranted to work toward the destruction of the old culture since it is neither Christian nor civilized. Thankfully, though, not all colonial-era missionaries were as rigid, which Chinua Achebe acknowledged by depicting another missionary who arrived before Reverend Smith. Mr. Brown, by contrast, is pictured trying to understand local customs and trying to help local people maintain their independence. He insists that Western education is necessary but only because without it, "strangers would come from other places to rule them. . . ."

The dichotomy between these two fictional missionaries serves as a useful tool for analyzing actual missionaries, which takes me back to David Livingstone, the original prototype and favorite punching bag for Marxists. What kind of missionary was he in his time?

A cultural imperialist, it would seem at first, especially to the critics who point to his first major discovery, the immense "Smoke that Thunders" waterfall on the Zambezi River. By renaming that cascade "Victoria Falls," he seemed to reveal where his real allegiance lay: with his earthly queen more than his heavenly king. And if there is any doubt, one has only to point to what he proclaimed after making this major geographical discovery—"Christianity, commerce, civilization"—a paradoxical mantra that remains stamped in bronze on the Zimbabwe side of the Victoria Falls, right where President Mugabe, one of the last diehard Marxist rulers in the world, has choreographed the complete ouster of white Rhodesian farmers.

For a while, when I was feeling especially shamed by my personal association with the Christian mission movement, I saw Livingstone as an example of everything gone wrong. To push him away was to protect myself, so I was quick to critique his naive blend of faith and capitalism: "Christianity, commerce, civilization." Obviously, it seemed to me, he had blazed a path for the English soldiers and settlers who followed, making it possible for them to command the entire region. Wasn't he, in essence, their colonial guide?

In all fairness, though, I have to point out that Livingstone was not just a stooge for the Empire. His deepest concern was for people being treated unjustly by Arab slavers—the very people Marx would have seen as an oppressed working class. He thought, wrongly or not, that if England entered Africa, encouraged by trading routes like major rivers, then the British would have to take a stand against Arab slavery. The Nile would bring Christian Westerners into the heart of the continent, where they would, hopefully, stop such injustice.

After witnessing the massacre of a whole village by Arab slavers, Livingstone called for immediate British intervention. After seeing the corpse of a woman speared and left to rot when she could no longer stay in file, he declared, "If my disclosures regarding the terrible Ujijian slavery should lead to the suppression of the East Coast slave trade, I shall regard that as a greater matter by far than the discovery of all the Nile sources together." Emancipation was his goal, in other words—not just geographic conquest.

Against the backdrop of other colonial opportunists, Livingstone actually seems a social saint. Take, for instance, the journalist Henry Morton Stanley, who made himself famous by clinging to the older man's coattails. After Stanley completed his famous trek to Lake Tanganyika, sent there by the *New York Herald* to determine whether Livingstone was still alive, he capitalized on the sudden fame and persuaded financiers to send him back into Africa, this time with a whole army of porters and hundreds of pounds of guns and ammunition. Unlike the missionary Livingstone, who had spent six years walking into villages with empty hands and open arms, Stanley basically shot his way across the continent east to west, killing natives preemptively in a kind of paranoid shock-and-awe approach to exploration. "The savage is impressed with nothing but force," he said in his book about the expedition. One of his disturbed competitors even claimed that Stanley had shot Negroes as casually as he shot monkeys.

No one was going to keep Stanley's heart and bury it in Africa. Nor were his few surviving porters going to carry his body back to England like they did with Livingstone. He had survived but only by sheer brutality, getting nicknamed "the one who breaks rocks."

In fact, as soon as he could make more profit from his accomplishments, he linked up with the most ruthless of the colonial rulers, King Leopold II, who sent him back up the Congo River to secure a huge tract of rainforest as his private money-making domain: the Belgian Congo.

My point is that capitalists and armies would have come to Africa anyway. The Empire would have stretched and grabbed. But the missionaries were sometimes, at their best, a conscience. Livingstone, unlike adventuring Stanley, was determined to stop the slave trade. And later, in the Belgian Congo, missionaries were the ones who began to send messages to the European press, reporting the atrocities of King Leopold's agents.

The most sympathetic of these missionaries knew that King Leopold's commerce was anything but Christian or civilized, and some had the courage to confront such injustice. For example, one outraged Baptist couple came back to Britain with eyewitness accounts of Belgian agents meting out a hundred lashes to villagers who had failed to gather the imposed quota of raw rubber: "Quickly the first defaulter is seized by four lusty 'executioners,' thrown on the bare ground, pinioned hands and feet, whilst a fifth steps forward carrying a long whip of twisted hippo hide. Swiftly and without cessation the whip falls, and the sharp corrugated edges cut deep into the flesh — on back, shoulders and buttocks blood spurts from a dozen places. . . ."

No, not all missionaries showed such fortitude. Even Studd, the famous cricket-playing founder of World Evangelization Crusade, was guilty of ignoring colonial abuses. When the Belgians in his area near the border of Sudan started cheating on taxes from local villagers, stamping incorrect dates on their receipts, Studd silenced a colleague who wanted to confront the corrupt agents. Fortunately, though, other missionaries *were* brave enough to risk their well-being for local people, such as the Baptist couple from England, the Harrises, who not only described the outrages but provided photos. They documented the whip scars on the bodies of those who couldn't meet the rubber quota, and the arm stumps of those who had lost hands, cut off as punishment for not harvesting enough of the wretched stuff. In one case, they even took a photo of a traumatized father staring numbly at the severed foot and hand of his five-year-old daughter.

This kind of witness, they felt, was their true Christian duty.

Twenty-One

strangely, I never did tell anyone about the gunner who had faked shooting at me with his mounted machine gun. I don't know why. Maybe I was embarrassed by how I had fallen to the floor cowering. Maybe I thought somehow I had asked for this reaction—or that it wasn't a big deal, given what others were going through. Anyway, I didn't feel comfortable admitting it, not even to Dan Coleman or my roommate Dave Iwan. Especially not to Dave.

Despite the fact that Dave was always padding up behind me in the dorm and putting me into a headlock, he was becoming a good friend. I had a lot of admiration for him because he seemed so cool and unaffected by all the threats around us. Not surprisingly, he was also a hunter par excellence. His slingshot was notched at least twenty times, representing kills. And he knew how to stuff birds taxidermy-style, which meant we had a lifelike lilac-breasted roller to enjoy right there in our dorm room, wings outstretched, lunging from its perch.

I was impressed every time I contemplated this open-winged roller, captured in the moment of taking flight. As far as I was concerned, this was the Holy Grail of East African songbirds, much more spectacular than its Kansas cousin. Whereas a scissor-tailed flycatcher in Kansas had a muted palette, limited to black and white, the lilac-breasted roller presented a battery of blues and purples that could put a peacock to shame. The big-beaked head was royal blue, the wings azure like a clean sky after rain. And on the breast, there was a striking patch of powdery lilac. In addition, two narrow electric-blue feathers framed the tail, sticking out like iridescent chopsticks.

To watch one of these winged wonders pursue an insect prey was a delight. First it would pump its way into the sky, pausing between flaps to stand on its pin-feathers. Then it would pirouette and dive.

And when it struck, the wings spread to full length, flashing pale blue as if a shard of sky had fallen.

All this I knew from memory, not from recent experience. And though I could recall seeing lilac-breasted rollers in the savannah back when I was seven or eight years old, I wanted to see one again. Not just the dead roller on our wall, stuck in its eternal pose, but a living bird showing off its powers.

So Dave, my hunting mentor, took me searching. After Yared drove us back from Good Shepherd Academy one afternoon, Dave led me into the eucalyptus forest below the school library, where he took potshots with his slingshot, ricocheting rocks off the trunks of trees. I didn't know if there were rules against hunting on campus, but he wasn't asking so I wasn't asking either. It felt good to be walking around with a weapon of sorts, turned dangerous.

As it turned out, we never did spot a roller, and I was secretly relieved because finding one might require killing one. Instead, we came upon some tiny cordon bleus with red-flecked cheeks, which scattered into the bushes. We also saw brown-crested mousebirds, which were busy raiding a neem tree on the other side of the fence. And we saw lots and lots of fat pigeons.

The latter, Dave said, were a general nuisance, pooping on roofs. He started to concentrate on them with his slingshot. One was particularly enticing, cooing high in an evergreen tree. It didn't realize the danger even after a shot whizzed by its branch, snickering into the eucalyptus forest. It bobbled its head and poked it out. Then Dave let loose again, and this time the stone struck it square in the neck. The bird fell like a beanbag, bouncing and sliding down the sloping branches of the evergreen. It plunked onto a bed of needles and, when we rushed up, it just lay there.

Another pigeon had clapped away, its wings beating madly, but this one was going nowhere. I felt shocked by the sudden stillness. Dave's big grin calmed me, however, demanding a different response.

"Nice shot," I exclaimed, my stomach tight inside me.

"Got lucky," he said. And he dug a hole with his heel to bury the gray-and-black bird with its glossy green neck. "No reason to stuff it," he said. "They're too common."

It seemed almost taboo—this arbitrary killing and burial. As if Dave had become a calloused assassin. However, though it seemed wrong, it also seemed edgy and exciting—like something I would want to do, something that would give me the kind of clout I had secretly wanted.

As soon as Dave toed the pigeon into the hole and covered it, I looked to the fence, where I noticed a soldier staring at us on the cobbled alleyway that led down to the stream and several shanties. He was just standing there with his eyes fixed on us, betraying no emotion—neither pleasure nor disgust, entertainment nor repulsion. Just flat scrutiny.

"Don't look at him, dope," Dave whispered. And he turned toward the dorm.

Reminded suddenly of the soldier who had faked firing a machine gun at me, I dropped my gaze and followed Dave, trying to seem as casual and as unaffected as he was. I felt all keyed up until we had gotten out of sight behind a building.

"What was with that guy?" I hissed.

"They're all like that, man. Trying to freak you out if they can."

The whole experience was astonishing really. That Dave could send a stone so straight and hard. That it could have such an abrupt effect, even bringing the soldier to a standstill. To have that kind of power—decisive and ultimate—was frightening but appealing. I wanted in on it. And so a few days later, Dave took me into the forest again, this time to make my own slingshot. We searched shrubs until we found a forked branch the right span for my grip. We cut it out of the bush with a pocket knife and stripped it until the "Y" of yellow wood was clean and smooth as dried bone. Then we whittled notches for tying on the rubber strips.

Dave donated the necessary surgical rubber, swearing that I better not waste it. Then he helped me to split the tube with a razor. We turned an old shoe tongue into a shooting pouch and carefully tied everything into place, checking to make sure the little bands held even when the pouch was yanked back. Unfortunately, shooting the contraption proved to be just as difficult as making it. The first time I released a stone, it barely flew a few yards, arcing into the ground.

"You're holding too stiff," Dave explained. "Swing your wrist down as you release." Then he let fly so hard that his rock pocked a hole in the bark of a nearby tree.

I tried to follow suit, but I flipped my wrist prematurely so that the back of my hand was where the pouch came through. The stone whacked my knuckles, forcing me to drop the whole thing in pain.

Dave grinned, his upper teeth showing their gap. "Not that far, you idiot."

For the next week, every time I arrived back from Good Shepherd, I went to grab my new slingshot and practice. I got closer and closer to my targets, but I couldn't hit one. Most frustrating were the flying kites that soared around our campus, alighting high in the eucalyptus forest. They seemed so large that I should be able to hit them in flight. However, they would see the stone coming and roll over or back-flap.

If Dave was with me, he would laugh. "Watch out, man. They might throw one back!"

I was jealous of the notches scoring his slingshot. Each represented a shot better than mine, and now I wanted to prove I had what it took. In frustration, I decided on a different tack altogether. If I couldn't shoot well with a slingshot, then I'd try another device— one that I had mastered back in Kansas. A bow.

I had been allowed to bring one of my two bows, since it was collapsible and small enough to fit into a footlocker. Its two metal halves slid together in the center handgrip, making it standard size. Since I had been shooting this thing for several years, I was convinced I could be more accurate. Maybe I would finally surprise Dave.

The only problem was how to keep a renegade arrow from flying over the school fence and impaling some unsuspecting pedestrian. Although these were only target arrows with dull metal tips, their piercing ability had become evident when I was shooting straight in the air and trying to get an arrow to drop back next to me. One of the high-climbing shafts drifted over our dorm and came down so hard it went right through the roof. Dave and I had to sneak into the attic through a trap door, to pull the arrow through the tin and patch the hole with a wad of gum.

After that incident, I knew I couldn't risk even more dangerous horizontal shots, so I was on the verge of putting the bow away. Then I remembered a few pictures I had seen in an outdoors magazine, with men shooting fish using arrows tied to a reel. In an attempt to mimic their approach, I tied a length of fishing line onto a target arrow and developed a technique for coiling the line at my feet. It worked fine enough, except that I had to be alert when the arrow hit the end of the line and came snapping back. I developed a side-step technique, as a result. Aim. Shoot. Step aside and watch the arrow whiffle past.

One afternoon, an Ethiopian boy about fourteen years old tracked me down the fence, mimicking my every move as I crept along, looking for feathered prey. Still in his blue school shorts and sweater, he crouched just like me and pulled an imaginary string back as if aiming at an imaginary prey. Then he clutched the chain link and called in jerky English, "Hey, you, what arra you doing?"

I ignored him, even though I could feel his eyes on me. I hadn't asked for his interruptions, which seemed incredibly rude.

A slender dove was roosting in an evergreen, perched low enough that I might get a reasonable shot. Doves were smaller than pigeons, and very elegant in their neat gray suits. Dave had told me that they were especially good for eating.

So I tiptoed forward, still ignoring the boy's call—"Hey, you, my friend. . . ." I pulled the arrow back to the corner of my mouth, fingertips touching my lips. Quietly, I dropped the fishing line from my bow-holding hand so it lay coiled at my feet. Then I looked down the tip of the arrow to the pigeon and aimed a bit low, knowing the arrow would rise at such a short distance. I hoped to hit the biggest part of the bird—the breast—but if I missed, I knew the arrow would fly on toward the chain link where the boy was watching. I decided I would just have to trust the fishing-line tether.

As soon as I released, the arrow sped to its target with a soft *fffftt*. I thought I had missed because the dove took flight. However, it fell sideways, thrashing at the needled branches. Sure enough, when I raced up, I could see that the arrow was driven right through it. Success at last!

For a moment, the dove paused in its frantic flapping, wings open in a sprawl, and I relaxed, relieved to see that it was dying. The black glistening eye blinked. The wings retracted as if giving up on further action.

However, as I tried to lift the arrow out of the tree branches, untangling the fishing line, the impaled dove went mad, flailing so hard that the arrow was wrenched out of my hand. I watched the bird bang its way farther into the tree, dragging the line after it. I could hear the Ethiopian boy laugh and call to some friends in Amharic. Then I could hear the other boys running to join him, flip-flops slapping.

"Hey, ferengi," one of them called. "Why arra you shoot bird?"

I felt angry and sad and near to panic, torn between cursing at them or throwing a stone. What had I done? The theoretical target had become a real creature, and it was suffering. I needed to stop the pain, but how? When Dave shot the pigeon, it was dead by the time it hit the ground. What did you do if the bird was only wounded?

I couldn't see how to finish what I had started. Or, to be more honest, I didn't have the guts. Death was supposed to do its own work, wasn't it? Surely the bird wasn't meant to stare back at me and try so desperately to get away. If I pulled the arrow out, wouldn't the creature fly from my hands in panic? And what would the kids at the fence say if it got away or, worse, flew right over the fence? For that matter, what would the Ethiopian soldier think if he was still here, watching?

It was galling to be scrutinized at this moment of weakness, torn by indecision. I figured the Ethiopian kids would have no squeamishness about killing a bird, having helped to butcher chickens a dozen times. Judging from the nightly gunshots in their neighborhood, they were a lot more familiar with death than I. But here I was, pinned down by their mockery, listening as they called yet another friend to join them, forming a little viewing gallery.

The dove flapped tentatively, tugging on the ungainly arrow. As it twisted on the shaft, I couldn't stomach anymore so I turned and ran, hearing the Ethiopian kids break into a cacophony of hoots and laughter.

"Dave," I yelled as I came racing down the hall of the dorm. "Hey, man, I need your help. I shot a bird."

"Congrats," he replied, reclining on his bed with a book.

"But it's still alive."

He smirked, the leanness of his face making his mouth thin and hard. "Are you telling me you just left it there?"

"Yeah, it's on the arrow."

"You mean, you got one with the bow?"

I heard the uptick in his voice and for a moment I was reminded of my original desire to prove myself. I felt a glimmer of pride followed by another wave of embarrassment. "Yeah, man, except I don't know how to kill it."

He shook his head woefully. "You'll be lucky if it's even there." Then he flipped the long brown hair out of his eyes and rose. "So where do we go?"

Dave was impressed when he saw the dove still hanging on the arrow, moving its wings faintly as if flying in its sleep. He didn't waste any time reaching through the branches of the evergreen and pulling the creature off the arrow as if unskewering a shish kebab.

"Damn," he said, wiping the grass with his bloodied hand, and I flinched at this unexpected expletive.

"Hey, you, my friend. Whaddis your name?" called the boys at the fence. But Dave ignored them.

"So this is what you do," he said, and he locked the dove's head into his fist with the neck between two fingers and the body hanging down. "You just lift and . . . ta-da!" With a hard downward snap, he flicked the bird's body away. It hit the ground with a thud, and when he opened his hand, there was the beaked head.

"Hey, man, give me money," called the boys at the fence, and Dave rushed at them shouting, "Mininit lidgeoatch," the Amharic expression for "What is wrong with you kids?"

"You want to cook it?" he asked as he turned back, and I thought of the hole through the dove's middle, now full of clotted blood. I thought of the bruised breast from where it had struck the ground when Dave beheaded it.

"I guess not," I said. And he grinned. "Then I got an idea."

The boys were moving toward the fence, coming in close to view the headless corpse. They were completely unprepared when he pulled back his arm and sent the body whirling over the chain-link.

They scattered, yelling as the bird came pinwheeling toward them. All of them ran except an older boy whose burning eyes refused to be startled. After the feathery corpse plunked down, he lifted it by a wing. Nonplussed, he held it out to his side and stared at us as if to ask, "Is this all you can manage?" Then he whirled it back.

As we walked to the dorm that late afternoon—with the sun low over the distant mountains, sending out long, long shadows—I felt a mixture of strange feelings. Relief. Dread. Pride. Shame. Confusion. I had killed my first bird. Why, then, I wondered, did I not feel simple satisfaction?

Twenty-Two

uilding Christ's Kingdom—as my parents were trying to do under the violent regime in Ethiopia—required an extreme form of pick-up-your-cross-and-follow-me self-denial. It meant, in its most radical form, being willing to die, as opposed to being willing to kill. By contrast, firing a slingshot was a small way to experiment with an aggressive stance. As a teenage boy, shooting that little weapon had its attractions even though it left me conflicted. What justification could I give for trying to kill birds when I did not even need to eat them?

How much more difficult it was to decide upon the right stance with regard to the Marxist cadres and their revolution, especially when reminded of the direct commands of Jesus to love the enemy and turn the cheek and make peace. But of course those are the very reasons Marx had argued in his 1848 *Manifesto* that the wealthy used Christianity to expand their control and diminish the control of the poor. Notice, Marx pointed out, that good Christians are instructed not to fight back; they should forgive. Good Christians are not supposed to demand earthly justice since true justice will come later—in heaven. Good Christians are supposed to obey the authorities, too, since God has placed those leaders in charge.

Just look at the converted slaves in America, Marx might have argued. See how they are pacified by their inherited faith, singing about the afterlife as if that is all the reward they can expect while they go on performing the mule-work of capitalism:

> I looked over Jordan, and what did I see
> Coming for to carry me home?
> A band of angels coming after me,
> Coming for to carry me home.

Today, of course, we know that those same slaves were singing in code—about the underground railroad, the sweet chariot that would swing low and carry them to a safe place across the Ohio River, borderline of the slave territories, but I'm convinced Marx would not have been satisfied with that secret resistance. Only direct conflict could correct the system. Blood had to be spilt. In fact, he wrote to Abraham Lincoln from his exile in London, where he was working on the three-volume *Das Kapital*, and he stressed that the American Civil War, terrible as it was, held much more validity for the working classes than George Washington's earlier "Revolution."

"The workingmen of Europe," he wrote, "feel sure that, as the American War of Independence initiated a new era of ascendancy for the middle class, so the American Antislavery War will do for the working classes. They consider it an earnest of the epoch to come that it fell to the lot of Abraham Lincoln, the single-minded son of the working class, to lead his country through the matchless struggle for the rescue of an enchained race and the reconstruction of a social world."

It's confusing, this issue of violence. It still is for me after decades of wrestling with different sides of the matter. And it doesn't help to see how church leaders have, at critical times, become so caught up in petty moral behavior that they would stand by doing nothing. Take, for example, the ministers who dragged their feet when Martin Luther King Jr., a century after Lincoln, tried to resist racial discrimination in a respectful, nonviolent fashion. What to do with *that* sort of Christianity, which would place more emphasis on church attendance and hair length than the rights of a whole people?

Unfortunately, even in Ethiopia in the middle of a full-scale revolution, such petty morality was inescapable, and it was about to crop up in a most unexpected fashion, adding to my perplexity as an existential youth who was trying quite hard to be "a good Christian."

Twenty-Three

O ut of all the adults I was getting to know at boarding school, I felt especially at ease with one couple: the patient, laid-back pair who served as our dorm parents. The Maxsons seemed always ready to engage in conversation, whether passing in the hall or hosting me in their apartment along with the other kids studying algebra.

Mr. Maxson was a gentle fellow with a pocked face who had a very attentive way of listening. And Mrs. Maxson, who had survived polio as a child, was a jubilant woman who got around with leg braces and arm crutches. She played the cornet one-handed, leaning on a single crutch, and liked to shock us into wakefulness at 6:30 a.m., blasting reveille down the hallway. The effect was so alarming that, on the first occasion, I even stumbled out of my room half expecting to find a cavalry charge.

"Heard you played the trumpet," she said. "Next time you should join me!"

Six-thirty was the official waking time, as Mrs. Maxson explained, and I was invited at 7:00 to join morning devotions. Sleepy but happy to be included, I came to those daily devotions, and I was impressed by attendance. Virtually all my dorm mates came, even Phil, the wild New Zealander, and Esther, the equally wild American, who had been meeting each other in the neutral zone between the guys' and girls' wings, stealing kisses.

I was inspired to find myself with teenagers who shared such commitment. In Troy, I had been close to one or two guys who would talk about beliefs or maybe, if pressed, say an awkward prayer. Here, by contrast, it seemed everyone was not only open to spiritual discussion but disciplined about it. In fact, one evening after hanging out at Dan Coleman's house listening to albums and talking about everything from girls to God, Dan initiated the idea of getting together for our own weekly Bible study.

In Troy, I would have been anxious about such a plan, but here I felt so enthused that I asked if we could include my brother Nat and his friend Paul. After all, what better way to stay in touch with Nat, now that we rarely saw each other?

I felt pious about the new endeavor until we gathered for the first time. Then I became scandalized. My brother's buddy Paul had a knack for imitating birdsongs and making strange faces. To talk with him about Bible verses was to encounter twitching eyes or whistled trills. Also, Paul and Dan were constantly inventing new slang words, persuading me to use them even if I wasn't sure whether we should act so frivolously. A boring person was a "Slug Bean." A scoundrel was an "Old Sinner." A cool dude was a "Weed." Dan was *dess lidge*, Amharic for "Joy Boy." And I, with my tendency toward pessimism, was quickly dubbed *dross lidge*, named after the sludge that got burned off of gold in the refining fire.

Even more shocking, Dan would insist that right after we closed in prayer, we play one of his phonograph albums—as if rock and roll was a necessary benediction. In my Kansas home we had rarely listened to anything other than placid instrumental music. Pat Boone was rowdy. Dan's favorites, by contrast, were wild screaming stuff by KISS or spooky pieces by Iron Butterfly. I knew instinctively that my parents would not approve. In fact, Dan's own dad had threatened to throw his collection of albums down the outhouse pit.

The way we concluded each Bible study—with Dan playing another album at the highest decibels possible—seemed blasphemous next to the absolute silence my parents kept as they did their morning devotions, occasionally turning the filmy pages of their Bible. While we shouted along with the pounding music and Dan arched back at the waist for maximum ecstasy, I alternated between delight and hot guilt. This was not the way I had been taught to have a "quiet time."

In fact, my father had carefully coached me into a devotional habit back when I was thirteen and we went on a father-son camping trip, a kind of coming-of-age ritual that he kept with all three of his sons. In my case, I had chosen to camp at a local hideout in a wooded valley near the Missouri River, making exploratory runs to find old homesteads where settlers might have lived in the mid-1800s. And it was out there in the woods—up in a quiet cottonwood—that I began what became a daily habit: reading a chapter of scripture, pondering it, writing my own interpretation and "application," then praying silently. Doing my devotions was a completely noiseless activity, aside from the rustling of the crinkly onionskin pages. As a result, staring at album covers in Dan Coleman's thundering bedroom seemed utterly wrong.

The KISS cover was especially unsettling. All those men in black leather tonguing the air or spouting fire from their painted faces. I couldn't shake the thought that our missionary parents would be aghast if they came into the room. How could we turn from the Bible to such wicked images, knowing that many Ethiopian Christians had championed the scriptures at the risk of imprisonment? How could I scream along with KISS when our friend Sahle had been thrown in jail just for playing a gospel recording? Or when Waja, the dresser from Soddo, was in a prison camp carefully memorizing single pages of a Bible that had been ripped apart and left in the latrine as toilet paper?

Still, there was no escaping the fact that the KISS music got me excited. A roaring engine introduced my favorite song—with wheels squealing for traction. Dan leapt onto his bed, legs spread wide, head arched back. He clawed at the imaginary strings of an electric guitar stretched across his crotch. He screamed along, lowering his voice only a little after there was a loud knock.

Would his dad come in and tear the record off the phonograph? Would he march right out to the trash heap and crack it in half?

Disturbed though I was, I still loved that Dan did not divide Christianity from the world, pushing each to opposite corners as I might try to do. For him, being Christian didn't mean shutting out rock music or girls or laughter for that matter. He could be sacrilegious because he didn't take religion seriously; faith, yes, but not religion. And this was tremendously appealing. Whereas some of my friends back in Troy had begun to hold me at arm's length when talking about necking with a girlfriend or sneaking cigarettes, Dan didn't step away. I felt enlivened by his transparency. In fact, I began looking for more of the same during gatherings like the morning devotions at the dorm. Candid, open conversations, that's what I wanted. Truly frank reflections.

Unfortunately, however, our dorm devotions started to seem pre-scripted instead, limited to the format in a book Mr. Maxson read. After weeks of rising early, one morning I was just too tired. In Kansas, I had always been the last one out of bed, jumping into clothes as my brothers sat in the running car, honking the horn. It was remarkable that I had lasted this long, arriving in the lounge by 7:00 a.m. each morning.

I couldn't pull back the covers. When I looked at the still gray light in the window, I couldn't find the willpower to strip in the cold air or to pad down to the shower. If only I could sleep for twenty more minutes. . . .

I missed the meeting again a few days later. Then it happened again. I wasn't trying to skip intentionally, and I didn't have any sense of wrongdoing. After all, I was still keeping my own daily devotions before bed. Plus, I was meeting each Wednesday evening with Dan and Nat and Paul for Bible study. However, one afternoon, after pretty much abandoning the morning devotions, I came home from Good Shepherd to find a note on my pillow, which read to this effect:

> Dear Tim,
> I am saddened by your refusal to join the community for devotions. I had hoped it would not come to this, but I feel I cannot remain silent any more, since your rebellion affects not only you but the others in the dorm. Imagine how they feel when you persist in "doing your own thing," disdaining the opportunity to start the day with Christ. Christ calls us to come aside and to open ourselves to Him. We all need to do this daily. In the future I expect to see you in the lounge promptly at 7:00 a.m.
>
> Sincerely,
> Jack Maxson

He had completely misunderstood. I was embarrassed to even consider how he saw me. From his perspective I must have appeared to be an intentionally difficult reprobate, while on the contrary, I was probably one of the least jaded teenagers he would meet. In Troy no one told me when to report for devotions. Nor was anyone telling me to go down to Dan's house every Wednesday evening. And hadn't his wife made the devotions seem optional when describing them?

There was something so wrong about this reprimand that it turned everything into a sham after that. I still liked the Maxsons very much. I wanted them to like me as well. But this reprimand lowered the very thing it claimed to elevate—shrank my eagerness into reluctant obedience. Now, when I wrestled myself into clothes and stumbled to the lounge, I went without any of the willingness that had made the exercise meaningful. When I looked at the others, I wondered if maybe they, too, were attending out of duty, not desire. I thought I could see, here and there, a kind of dull fixation in their eyes.

As for me, my mind was definitely slipping away, attaching to anything but the scriptures: the curve of a girl's breast, the smell of ashes in the fireplace, or the hope that Dave Iwan would take me slingshot-hunting in the woods behind our dorm. Although Waja and Ethiopian Christians were waking in the prison camps of the Derg, committing their own quiet rebellion by memorizing chapters of the Bible, now I was rebelling by refusing to concentrate.

Twenty-Four

The main criticism coming from missionaries in Ethiopia with regard to the Orthodox church has always been simple: legalism. They look at the long-standing structure of that state church—freighted with fifteen centuries of accumulated customs—and lament the way it drifted off course, emphasizing human rules over God's grace. To this day, children from Orthodox families start daily church school as young as five, memorizing prayers and psalms in the medieval liturgical language, Ge'ez. Although they might not know what they are saying, they will recite the prayers and psalms over and over like an incantation, setting the stage for a lifelong observation of rote worship. Over thirty thousand of those church schools exist, according to the official Web site of the Ethiopian Orthodox Church, and adults who have been trained into the church are expected to recite the same memorized prayers daily, following a strict set of rules: standing first, putting on a belt-like "girdle," facing eastward, making the sign of the cross, kneeling, then prostrating with face to the floor.

Orthodox believers are also expected to fast on designated holy days (250 for the more ambitious, but at least 180 days a year for an average member), to participate in religious parades on feast days set aside for saints, to send their children to traditional church school, to pay a priest tax, and give alms to the poor (who gather at the church entrance, knowing that true believers will have to respond out of religious duty just as true Muslims do at mosques).

To the watching Protestant, such rule-bound behavior doesn't seem very different than the behavior of the Pharisees, the Jewish rule-keepers in Jesus's time. Jesus criticized the Pharisees for wearing wide, noticeable phylacteries, which were leather "scripture boxes" strapped to the forehead as a reminder to pray. Jesus criticized them for fussy laws about tithing: "Woe to you, teachers of the law and Pharisees, you hypocrites. You give a tenth of your spices—mint, dill, and cumin. But you have neglected the more important matters of the law—justice, mercy, and faithfulness . . ." (Matthew 23.23–24).

Raised in evangelical circles where such conduct was condemned, I naturally suspected anyone from a liturgical church, whether Orthodox or Roman Catholic. Those "ritualistic Christians" were, in my mind, misguided apostates who had fallen prey to their own legalism. We, by contrast, were grace-oriented resisters—aptly labeled "Protestants" because we had bucked a false system and returned to the true teachings of Jesus. Whereas they kept the letter of the law, we kept the spirit. Whereas they were Pharisees, we were disciples.

It took me another decade to acknowledge just how pharisaical we could be, too—with our morning devotions and weekly Bible studies, our modest clothing and cleaned-up language, our ban against alcohol and cigarettes, our expectation of baptism and monthly tithes, even our exclusive separatist schools.

Evangelicals are not exempt by any means from the inherent problems that go with organized religion. When humans coalesce, rules are required. And though the missionaries of my youth critiqued the idea of earning one's way into heaven through prescribed "good works," they were susceptible to that same way of thinking, deeply concerned with obedience, first to God and then to the leaders who, as ministers or church elders, represented God. They were, more than most Christians from mainstream denominations, concerned with who was "in" or "out," meaning in essence, who was damned or saved. And they wanted a clear way to measure the difference: here's proper Christian behavior or there's suspect behavior.

Of course, I wanted the same clarity myself. It's natural to wish for surety—to be utterly convinced. However, today I still carry a knot of sustained resentment down in my gut; that is, with regard to the strict inconsequential rules we maintained at Bingham Academy and the implicit message that if we were just disciplined enough, we would be chosen by God.

Let me be clear, though. This is not an exposé of my dorm parents per se. The Maxsons were good people who were simply doing their expected work as part of a larger legalistic system. I was too, as I knuckled under and started to attend devotions regularly. I think we were all misguided together, trying terribly hard to do what was right, to live in an exemplary, Christ-like fashion. In my own sincerity I was convinced that the Pharisees were out there on the other side of the fence, safely removed. It never occurred to me that they might be right in our own community or even staring back in the mirror.

Twenty-Five . . . .

n March, after more than two months apart from us, Mom finally flew to Ethiopia, having arranged for her mother to be transferred to her brother's house. When Dad fetched Nat and me for an overnight at Headquarters, she hugged us fiercely. Over dinner, she explained that Grandmother had gained back her memory and was getting by without a walker, shuffling from place to place in her old familiar way. Now that her house was for sale, all that remained of her past life were a few heirlooms Mom had shipped to the West Coast.

I imagined Grandmother in a guest bedroom in Seattle, waiting each afternoon for her son to return from work. I imagined her hearing the slow tocking of the grandfather clock, which had accompanied her there, beginning its long migration in 1794, all the way back in Reading, Pennsylvania, then traveling to Kansas, and now to the Pacific Ocean.

"Will Grandma know anyone except Uncle Paul?" I asked.

Mom sighed and told me that, no, Grandmother would be starting over, but thankfully she got along nicely with a neighbor lady. Also, Mom said, Grandma was enthused about a sliding door that opened onto the backyard, where she hoped to watch birds at the feeder and pray. "She's a prayer warrior, you know. And she's going to pray every morning for each of us. Johnathan, too, up in Illinois."

The reminder of my grandmother's love for birds made me feel bad about my hunting exploits, which had become routine after the initial shock of killing a dove. But I didn't dwell on that because I was even more struck by the mention of my brother Johnathan, whom I had practically forgotten. How could that be? How could I have been so unaware of my older brother since coming out here to Ethiopia?

Mom talked about what Johnathan was studying in his second semester at Wheaton College. He was doing well but seemed awfully busy. We should pray that he not get too stressed, she insisted, and she said this with more than a casual emphasis.

I have a big brother, I thought. And he is having a hard time of some sort. I prayed for him internally, trying to imagine where he might be at the moment. Eating lunch in a cafeteria? Running across a lawn between brick buildings?

Then I drifted back to where I was standing—in the guestroom where Mom and Dad were staying, and where Nat and I would sleep for the night, squeezed onto cots behind a cloth screen. Nat and I undressed and slid under the cold sheets. And just before we fell asleep, Dad added one more major bit of news from the other side of the screen. He announced that the director of the mission, Mr. Cumbers, had assigned our family to Bulki station in the deep south, the same place where Waja had opened his pharmacy before being arrested and carted off to prison camp. In fact, Dad and Mom would be flying there in a few days, and we would join them during our upcoming Easter break.

I was surprised by this development, having begun to think that the mission would keep Dad in Addis, where he was virtually their only doctor. I was also a bit unsettled because during our one visit to Bulki twelve years ago, although I had loved riding a mule up the mountain seated behind Mom, I was traumatized when local farmers began burning their fields.

As they had started those field-clearing fires far below the mission compound, I watched with toddler curiosity, fascinated by the twisting lines of flame that wriggled up the slopes. I had tried to evade my mandatory nap, but Mom forced me to lie down and sleep, and when I woke I was startled by smoke all around me, so much of it that I could see a gauzy haze against the ceiling. Hearing shouts on the lawn, I ran to the main room of the bungalow, staring under the middle slat of the screen door, and I was alarmed to see that the field-burning fires had advanced all the way to the tin-walled clinic where my father was working just fifty yards away.

On that afternoon long ago, the wind on the crest of the mountain breathed new life into the crawling flames, lifting them so that a cluster of eucalyptus saplings suddenly burst, their oily leaves igniting with a whoosh. And terror took over as my mother ran to the line of fire, stomping at low-lying flames and smacking the ground with a eucalyptus branch. When Dad jogged out of the clinic to help her and patients hobbled onto the charred grass hacking, I formed the impression that everything was going to be destroyed: the clinic, the bookshop with its translated gospels, the gardens, and the little mountaintop bungalows with their whitewashed walls. Us too.

More than a decade later, I knew that I had overreacted, but I still couldn't help feeling a twinge of old alarm. "How safe is the Bulki area?" I asked from where I lay on my cot behind the cloth screen.

Mom replied that it was probably one of the least affected stations in terms of the revolution. Yes, it was not far from where Waja was arrested, but there hadn't been much trouble otherwise, and Mr. Cumbers thought that the area was too removed to get much attention from the government.

"It's really sort of a frontier," she said, describing how several Wolaittan evangelists were working in the valley below, trying to sway members of an untouched tribal group.

"Down there, things are a bit more dicey," Dad added, not able to hide the fascination in his voice as he described an old initiation custom that some of the men observed—requiring a boy to prove himself by killing someone from a rival tribe. "No killing, no marriage!"

Then Mom broke back in, "But, Charles, that's way below the mountain where we'll be staying, right? It's more peaceful in the highland areas."

This was a lot to absorb at ten at night in a cot in revolutionary Addis Ababa. Living on a mountain so remote that there was no road? Eating meals cooked on a woodstove? Doing it all within thirty or forty miles of people who still believed you had to kill to prove your manhood?

While I slowly drifted off to sleep, I contemplated the fact that we would be living beyond the edge of where most missionaries lived, which made me nervous but strangely enthused. The next day, I would enjoy telling my roommate Dave. No doubt, in a place like Bulki there would be all sorts of wildlife, including birds to hunt—the sort that Dave was always talking about when letting me know that our school compound was lousy for hunting.

As it turned out, I didn't really get a chance to tell my roommate about Bulki until late the next day, after taking the usual set of classes and busing across Addis Ababa to watch the Good Shepherd basketball team play our arch-rival, the American School. Then, because Good Shep was winning and everyone was screaming with anticipation, Dave was too distracted to shout much more than, "You lucky dog! You'll be able to hunt all over that place."

Good Shepherd won the game, outlasting a stripped-down team of diplomat teens and company kids whose parents had not heeded the State Department's warning to leave Ethiopia. And because this was our traditional rival, we learned that there would be a "victory party" on Friday. The city-wide curfew had been lifted, so we might even stay late if we could convince Mr. Maxson.

"It's actually going to be a dance," Dave confided when we got back to the dorm. "But don't call it that. When we talk to the Maxsons, it's just a party, right?"

I nodded.

"And don't tell Stamp. If he finds out, he'll feel like he has to report it."

Already I had gathered that Brad Stamp was the appointed "square" in the Bingham hostel, always sitting up properly, backbone stiff as a soldier's, dressed in button-down shirts rather than the T-shirts the rest of us took as uniforms. I felt sorry for him because he seemed so separate from everyone else, but I said nothing about the upcoming party when I saw him in the hallway. I didn't want to be the snitch who jeopardized the fun.

To my surprise, on that Friday evening, Brad still showed up on the periphery of the group waiting for Mr. Maxson to fetch the van. I wondered if maybe he had accidentally heard about the "party" without realizing it was a dance. Shouldn't we tip him off?

Not me, though. I didn't want the possible repercussions.

"Thank the Lord for Lutherans," Dan Coleman muttered as we waited, voicing his appreciation for the liberal faculty at Good Shepherd who were sponsoring this gathering. Then, as Mr. Maxson pulled up, he whispered another jibe: "So, dross lidge, do you know why Baptists don't make love standing up? . . . No? Because it might lead to dancing."

I choked back a laugh, conscious of Brad just behind me, not join-

ing in the laughter. Then I piled in with the rest and joined the gabfest
that broke out as we were waved through two checkpoints in a row,
not having to come to a stop.

Mr. Maxson called out: "So do you guys want me to stay for
this deal?" And you could hear the edge in Dave Iwan's voice as he
shouted back over the top of all our voices: "You'd have to wait awfully long."

"I heard it's not over until 11:00," added Dave's older brother, who
was a senior and had just the right tone of authority.

Mr. Maxson had to negotiate. "Not that late! I'll come back, but
right at 10:30. You're just lucky the curfew isn't in effect now."

The first thing I noticed once we dashed inside the classroom that
doubled as a dance floor was the low lighting. That and the fact that
Gladys Knight and the Pips were playing on the phonograph. A girl
from Good Shepherd was dancing alone. In the past, she had seemed
boyish and tough to me with her low voice and cropped raven hair.
But tonight she was wearing a tight white top, and the way her body
shimmied made her anything but boyish.

The songs that followed were tame—Neil Diamond, ABBA, Paul
McCartney and Wings—but the secretive nature of the whole event
made it quite thrilling. If being policed by the Bingham staff could
be frustrating, the flip side was that resisting felt delicious. A few
of the bolder members of our hostel took to the dance floor right
away. Phil and Esther were not shy, shaking their hips to the center of
everything. Dan glided out too, holding hands with his girlfriend. But
Stamp, as expected, stayed on the perimeter looking troubled, and I
was stuck nearby, hovering next to the chips as the girl I had once
hoped to date—Mari Dye—pulled her boyfriend into action.

At the few school dances I had attended in Troy, I had been with
a cluster of friends who, like me, were not attached. Even though I
was reluctant to actually dance, I had gotten support from the sidelines—guys who would push me onto the floor if a girl initiated or
who would help me get up the nerve to ask someone. This new situation gave me a near panic attack. I knew no one well, aside from Dan
and Dave. Most of the girls from our hostel were already spoken for,

so I had to either hide or break through my shyness. To my surprise, I suddenly decided to go right up to a Good Shepherd girl whom I had greeted only once or twice and to simply ask, "Hey, want to dance?"

Crossing that busy floor was like walking down the high diving board, determined to try a flip. I feared it could be disaster. All I knew about this girl was that she was the daughter of our Bible teacher, Mr. Brown, and that she had great hair. It was light-brown hair, a wonderful thick mane that rested on her shoulders. Since she stood alone on the edge of the party just like me, she seemed like she might be open for something to happen.

Unfortunately, she just shook her brown tresses, arms crossed over her chest.

Now what?

When you reach the end of the diving board and take that last big step, stopping is awkward. It means going into a squat and waving arms. And if you turn to walk away, you know that the whole swimming pool could be watching.

I asked again, "C'mon, just one dance?"

She giggled, which I took as a positive sign. I didn't even know if I liked her. There was a certain stiffness to her, as if she wasn't sure how safe it was to move. Nonetheless, I took one last running leap and pitched forward off the board. "Why not?" I asked.

She looked away and seemed to take a deep breath. She glanced back, this time more seriously, almost mad. "Look," she seemed to be saying, "this isn't easy." Then she rolled her eyes and uncrossed her arms, taking a step toward me. And finally we were out there together, smiles taped into place, kicking the floor and swinging our arms. We were dancing and feeling good about it. At least I was.

After that initial dance, we danced again. We even tried a slow dance, holding each other neither close nor far away, her breasts brushing my chest and sending electric surges down my front. Having broken through our awkwardness, we hung out the rest of the party at the punch bowl, talking about where we had lived, who we knew, what we liked to do. We talked for about forty minutes, standing just a few feet away from silent Brad, who had never danced at all and who slid his folding chair against the wall.

I still wasn't sure if I really liked this girl, but I was elated to have conquered my own fear. I was elated as well to not think about anything dark or dire for a while. No kebele checkpoints or AK-47s or prisoners unjustly held in labor camps. Not even Bulki station with its nearby tribe of men who had to kill to prove themselves. Just this loud noise in a warm room with people bouncing around. And for a bit, complete freedom from the serious guy in my head who was usually muttering, "You know, you're looking like a fool."

As 10:30 approached, my roommate posted himself at one of the shuttered windows, opening it enough to peek out. Suddenly he whistled and jerked an arm toward the door. I said good-bye then dashed into the cool night air, where stars were glittering. I clambered into the van with the rest, who were all chattering.

"How was the party?" Mr. Maxson shouted.

"It was a blast. Totally cool," we yelled back.

Then from the rear of the van, where he had taken his seat on the spare tire, Brad Stamp spoke for the first time all night: "Nobody told me it was to be a dance!"

"Dance?" Mr. Maxson asked.

By our shocked silence we were damning ourselves, so we all started talking at once, trying to deny, explain, or do anything that might distract Mr. Maxson. But the damage was done. By the time we got back to the parking lot at Bingham Academy, we had received the official proclamation: no more "victory parties."

As we went up the ramp into the dorm that evening, stumping down the hallway, we all stared sharply at the stiff shoulders of silent Brad. I felt bad about how we had kept him in the dark, but I was mad, too. He seemed so detached that I wondered if he could even understand why these dances were important to us. Did he ever let himself go—just enough to enjoy the freedom of the moment? Did he ever stop policing himself and everyone else?

That night in bed, I replayed the first moment on the dance floor, when I had convinced Mr. Brown's daughter to join me—the moment when we had begun to stomp and spin to the ABBA song "Bang-A-Boomerang." No question, it had been worth it. What a release—almost as if I'd taken off a leaden vest and returned to my true weight. That's what I would miss now, every time our Good Shepherd friends told us that there was going to be another victory party. I dozed finally, hearing high-pitched harmonies but feeling a strange apprehension, as if some cat burglar could pick the lock and steal the songs away. Hadn't King David danced, I thought, recalling a time when he came home from defeating the Philistines with the Ark of the Covenant at the head of his procession? Hadn't he even taken to the streets half-naked, rebuking the woman who told him he was acting like a fool? And if David could dance, then why couldn't we?

Twenty-Six

know, what in the world did that last chapter have to do with the Ethiopian revolution?

A lot, though.

Just like there is a tension between heaven and earth (at least for the evangelical Protestant), there is a tension between body and soul. And just like heaven trumps earth, soul trumps body.

To go further, for most evangelicals the body is not trustworthy. It stands in the way of the soul—distorts, obscures, confuses, distracts, seduces. The body is a dumb mass of animal drive, and the soul, trapped inside that reckless vessel, lives in constant tension, at risk of ruin.

Today, I attend a church where the body is not so divorced from the soul—a church that has a sacramental theology receptive to the life we lead as physical beings. But when I was sixteen my body was a danger zone I could not escape, pulling me into humiliating conflict with my assumptions about proper Christian conduct. I felt the tension right down into the core of my bones, into my entrails, and, more than anywhere else, into the fickle blood-muscle-prong of my sex. And so, even though Joan, the daughter of my Bible teacher, seems a major tangent in this "war story," she's not. She reveals the battle that was raging inside myself, between soul and body, which is quite related to the battle outside myself, between heaven and earth—at least as I experienced it when I was still the conflicted teenage son of Baptist missionaries.

That heated internal tension was due, in no small part, to the near-paranoid caution of the mission when it came to sexuality. Until the late 1960s the Bingham faculty had enforced a six-inch rule, which kept all males and females physically apart. Dancing was absolutely prohibited. Cassettes were confiscated if deemed too provocative.

The school librarian even went through each magazine and cut out photos that showed too much skin, so that whole sections were riddled with square and rectangular holes where ads had promoted questionable products such as bras or suntan lotion or soap.

How do I know this last fact? Because I went flipping through those same magazines, unable to resist the siren song of my raging hormones even though the exercise was futile and left me feeling irritable as a leashed cat. I was not aware that this drive was very natural nor that I was probably suffering from being alone, cut off from my family and familiar community. No one had told me that I was moving out of one developmental stage into another—from adolescence into what the psychologist Erickson described as young adulthood—a time characterized by a crisis between intimacy and isolation.

I doubt any of us, as missionary children, realized just how normal we were back then, and certainly not Brad Stamp, who had, as I discovered twenty years later, struggled so mightily with the need for intimacy that he had taken to peeping through a window to watch girls undress, something I might have done myself if I had made many more of those frustrating trips to the school library. It was Dan Coleman who told me about Brad years later, explaining that one Sunday evening before I arrived from Kansas, Brad got up and made a tearful public confession during the church service at mission headquarters, unburdening himself of the inner, acid-like fire of his sin.

For Karl Marx, by contrast, sex was no more than a biological necessity, a cause for procreation. He did not comment on the topic much aside from prostitution, which he believed turned women into victims of a capitalist system. It took his protégé, Engels, to fully apply Marxist theories to sexual relations, pointing out in the 1880s how men controlled all labor and property rights, demanding a subservient fidelity from women, who were treated as yet another form of property. In other words, Engels argued, women were victims (like the proletariat) of the property-owning class, and they would have to rise up too, asserting their rights.

Of course, I didn't have an inkling of such gender politics when I was in Ethiopia, where the evangelical church movement seemed quite progressive to me. Ethiopian evangelicals were bringing new rights to women who had always been treated as voiceless members of the society, cloistered in the home, where they were expected to birth babies and do domestic chores. Evangelicals were opening the door for women to go to school and to hold jobs, including jobs that demonstrated equal intellectual ability. But, to be honest, I am not sure I even noticed or cared about such matters. I just knew I wanted to be connected to a girl and that trying to connect made me feel out of control, no longer the reasonable mind-over-matter being that I thought I should be.

What I was learning was that if one shuns the body for too long, shoving it away, away, away, then it will wait for the most inelegant moment to lunge back, taking its embarrassing revenge. Thought you were loyal to a higher spiritual cause? Think again. Thought you had something transcendent to offer to the world—a kind of exemplary way of life that you could recommend over the messy material life of nature? Think again, you hypocrite.

That was the voice I heard increasingly, hissing in my head as I tried to be a better Christian, the sort of believer who would take a stand in the world just like the missionaries and Ethiopian converts I admired.

Twenty-Seven

J oan, the girl who danced with me, had apparently been smitten. She kept appearing unexpectedly, seeking me out. Since I had told her about not feeling challenged by the music we were playing in band, which was much more rudimentary than songs we played in Troy, she brought me sheet music from a storage closet at Good Shepherd, where she had access because of her father, Mr. Brown. Then she brought me a whole book of trumpet tunes by Herb Alpert and the Tijuana Brass.

The fact that she had borrowed this book without telling anyone was unsettling. Even more disturbing was the fact that the cover sported a dark-haired beauty seated on the floor in what appeared to be a flowing dress with a low-cut bodice but on closer examination turned out to be nothing more than whipped cream. Her come-hither eyes called to me. She had dipped one finger in the cream, and she held that finger to her parted lips.

Every time I pulled out this book of sheet music in my dorm, presumably to practice on my trumpet, there was that seductive siren looking back in a way that made me severely compromised. I wondered, was Joan so naive that she didn't realize the innuendo of what she had given me? Then I wondered, even worse, was I so naive that I didn't realize what Joan intended?

At night, after the lights were out, the Tijuana Brass cover flickered into my mind. I tried to say bedtime prayers as gunshots rattled in the distance, but all I could picture was swelling cleavage rising out of whipped cream. Lord, protect me, I prayed. Keep me from temptation. Then I succumbed and reached under the blankets to caress myself, going against the biblical warning that flashed in my head blood-red: "I tell you, anyone who looks at a woman lustfully has already committed adultery. . . ."

As soon as the shivers of pleasure had subsided, I was swept by a wave of sulfurous shame. I had failed to stay pure. I had willfully disobeyed one of God's commandments—Do not covet. Who knew? Maybe this Tijuana woman was even married to someone, which meant I was an adulterer.

When I passed the daughter of my Bible teacher the next morning, walking between classes, my face burned. To see her hopeful smile was to be reminded of my own sinfulness, all the more so because I now knew I had danced with her not out of attraction but out of a need to overcome my own timidity.

For a while, I expected lightning to strike, delivering a deserved judgment. But it never came. Then I began to notice another quieter girl at Good Shepherd who had not even attended the dance—a girl who was a year younger and had only one class with me. Nancy had an alert poise. She never said much, but her clear gray eyes sparkled when I greeted her. The more she smiled, the more I smiled.

I didn't have the nerve to initiate anything this time. My attempts at romance had backfired twice, first with Mari Dye and then Mr. Brown's daughter. So why add to the list? Still, I couldn't help asking Nancy, when all of the kids at the Bingham hostel decided to host an open house for friends at Good Shepherd, whether she might be coming, and I felt elated when she nodded shyly.

On the day itself, she stayed close by me at the dorm, engaging in playful banter. She also hung back after the others had gone out the main door headed to the dining hall, where we would watch a film about John Wayne as a tough one-eyed marshall helping a girl track down the man who murdered her father. There was no way for me to get even a moment alone with Nancy, since Mrs. Maxson shooed us out of the dorm. But as we followed the crowd toward the improvised movie theater, I noticed she did not try to get back to the safety of her friends. She walked close enough that her shoulder bumped mine.

I bumped her back and she laughed. I felt we had an agreement of some sort. Emboldened by this small contact, I suddenly did something uncharacteristically impulsive. After checking that no one was looking, I reached for her hand and pulled it into my jacket pocket, ecstatic to feel her fingers slipping together with mine in a secret tryst.

When she smiled and tightened her grip, the supple warmth of her fingers was as sensuous as anything I'd experienced.

In that quiet way the two of us became a couple and began to open up about our families and pasts. I learned that her parents were Presbyterian missionaries who worked with the Anuak and Nuer people, relatively untouched tribes in one of the toughest regions of Ethiopia—a hot, muggy lowland near the Sudanese border. At the time I didn't even know that her town of Gambela was where Dr. Lambie had come across the border in the early 1900s, starting the Ethiopian branch of our mission. All I knew was that the river there had gotten a flash of attention when the international press reported a Peace Corps volunteer torn to pieces by an exceptionally large crocodile. Nancy said that after that moment of macabre attention, the whole region had fallen off the map, although she and her family still went fishing near the same place where the attack occurred. She liked to boast about crocodiles and hippos she had seen, and about the monster fish she caught.

"You know," she told me and Dave Iwan during one lunch break, "last Christmas I caught a Nile perch that weighed fifty pounds."

"Yeah, and I used to have a cat the size of a horse," I replied. But I had to eat crow when Dave Iwan confirmed that Nile perch could weigh much more than fifty pounds, even a hundred and fifty.

Nancy lifted a sleeve and flexed her bicep in victory. She got all feisty whenever she was talking about things she loved to do back at Gambela, not just trolling the hot muddy river but making ice cream in a hand-churned bucket or playing with her dog Fifi. She spoke of her life there as if it was the best of lives. Other girls might be resentful about giving up air conditioning and shopping malls, but Nancy seemed genuinely pleased about having a home on the edge of nowhere.

She didn't have to talk all the time either. If I had arranged with Yared to take the later bus with the basketball team, the two of us would loiter under a eucalyptus tree, communing in our own telepathic way. The dry season was just starting to give way to the rainy season, so showers would fall suddenly, forcing us to take shelter under the eaves of the classrooms. There was something delicious about just huddling there, saying nothing while the rain fell in a torrent, drumming on the tin and streaming off the edge in a see-through sheet. We watched, mesmerized, feeling the mist on our skin. When I lifted one arm around her shoulders, I could hardly bear the pleasure that came from her warmth against my ribs, the caress of her fine brown hair on my elbow.

Those early rains were short. Once they stopped, the sun tended to crack back through the scudding clouds, sending light flickering. It shone on the puddles. It lit the clean grass, every blade flashing pure green and silver. Dripping with light, the trees shed their remaining water, and we sat enthralled. For a while we forgot that Ethiopia was going to ruin beyond the fence. We also forgot that some of the university students who had cheered when Emperor Selassie was toppled were now beginning to mount new protests, frustrated by Mengistu's regime.

One afternoon, however, when the sky was clear and Nancy and I went walking along the furthest edge of campus, admiring the wide-open sweep of the plain and blue foothills in the distance, we were brought out of our shared reverie by a crescendo of automatic rifle fire. We froze, staring back across campus. The clamor of those machine guns did not fluctuate in the run-and-hide bursts we usually heard at nighttime. We felt exposed standing by a flimsy chain-link fence, so we raced for the center of the school, where we found all the other students gathered by the cafeteria.

The shots stopped finally, and Yared arrived with our bus, which made everyone more relieved, but I could tell he was agitated, and on the way back to Bingham, as he swung the bus around potholes, he explained that some of the university protesters had marched right to Revolution Square to shout their frustration under the massive portraits of Marx, Engel, and Lenin. Then the government soldiers had opened fire. He said that at least a hundred protesters were shot. He also said soldiers had dragged away their bodies without letting parents identify them.

The next morning, as Yared shuttled us to Good Shepherd and back, he continued his rumor reports, murmuring to Dan and me that a friend of his had seen soldiers use a bulldozer to dig what looked like a mass grave, unloading trucks into the hole. According to his friend, this grave was on the same side of Addis as Good Shepherd. It was out there in the blue hazy foothills that Nancy and I had admired as we were walking.

A few more days passed and Yared told us that now several leaders of the student protests had been executed. Supposedly, their parents had not been allowed to take the bodies until they paid for the bullets. Yared told us also that there were high schoolers marching with these university protesters, so it seemed likely that some of the executed were our own age. Sixteen, like me. Or fifteen, like Nancy.

The horror of this new violence, directed at fellow teenagers, seemed doubly intense. It was magnified by the absence of our parents, who were living hours away by airplane. When Nancy and I came together at Good Shepherd once again, I felt hyper-aware, completely in the moment. A heavy rain fell, and afterward I became fixated on a rosebush flaring out of the ground near to the roofed walkway where we sat. I gazed so closely at the leaves of that rosebush that I saw individual raindrops beaded on the waxy surface. I saw droplets trickle into an opening bud, nestling in the velvet creases. A light perfume lifted off the thick white petals, sweet as honeyed meringue, and I marveled that a scent could be so singular, so pure. I pulled Nancy in closer, not sure what tomorrow would bring, but thankful that we were at least alive.

Fire and Sky

On the morning of the third day there was thunder and lightning,
with a thick cloud over the mountain, and a very loud trumpet blast.
Everyone in the camp trembled. Then Moses led the people out
of the camp to meet with God, and they stood at the foot of the
mountain. Mount Sinai was covered with smoke, because the LORD
descended on it in fire. . . .

EXODUS 9.16−19

Twenty-Eight

When Easter holiday arrived just a few weeks later —in April of my sophomore year—my mother and father flew into Addis so they could take Nat and me to our new station, traveling on one of the single-engine Cessnas operated by Missionary Aviation Fellowship. Although I was reluctant to leave Nancy after such a short period, the flight was a wonderful release. Gone was the tension of being under siege inside fenced compounds or feeling menaced at checkpoints. Nat and I whooped as the English pilot let go of his follow-the-rules façade and buzzed low over a lake. "Take a gander," he shouted, as a flock of flamingos swerved away, painting a half-circle of pink.

Remarkably, the government had not stopped these flights, but there was a growing concern that the planes might be seized since other mission property was getting commandeered by the rural equivalent of the kebele, local associations called gebere, an Amharic term for "farmers." In fact, a station that the pilot had just pointed out ten minutes earlier was one of the first casualties of the new attitude toward missionaries. Soddo was where Dr. Lambie had sent the first team of missionaries to set up a station in 1927. It was where we lived when I was only three, and where Mari Dye wrote me when we were in Kansas. And now it was where the mission was getting a hard lesson about how gebere associations might treat other stations around the country. At Soddo local cadres had suddenly ejected all the missionaries, taking their furniture and appliances then turning the hospital over to doctors imported from Cuba. As if to press home the change in ownership, the new staff even painted a mural of Castro across the hospital entrance.

The relations with the geberes weren't improving either. More recently, in northern Ethiopia another one of these suddenly formed associations had arrested the father of a classmate, transporting him to a prison in Addis despite the fact that he was a well-respected doctor. When I asked my friend Stan Cannata what charges were given, he looked like he'd bit into a lime: "The usual crap. They said he was CIA. Their evidence was the shotgun we use for hunting. They took our two-way radio, too, because Dad was supposedly sending messages to the Amhara loyalists."

Now as our Cessna winged its way toward Bulki station, I thought about Stan's dad in prison, glad that we would at least be stationed in the south instead of in the northern regions where Amharas were fighting to bring back the monarch or where Tigrinya rebels were demanding a separate state. In the south there wasn't the same sort of open warfare, not unless you went to the eastern corner of the nation, where Somali raiders were attempting to wrest away a chunk of the Ogaden desert lost during World War II. Out there where Dave Iwan's parents lived, one of the other Sudan Interior Mission stations had been closed because guerrillas spilled onto the compound during a gun battle, holding a group of missionaries hostage for a day and night and treating the women in a manner that no one would talk about.

"But that's a long way from where we are headed," Dad had assured me when I brought up the incident.

"And thank God," Mom sighed, "no one was killed."

The Cessna rose to cruising altitude as we left the lake. Then the pilot opened a map across the front windshield. I felt like I ought to reach up and hold the U-shaped controls, which were rocking slightly. I looked at Nat with raised eyebrows, until he leaned over to shout, "Look, Ma, no hands." Then Mom glanced back from her seat, cocking her own brow.

"You two could use trims," she observed, grinning at the big bowls of hair we had grown. "You're three inches taller, but it's all hair."

We just smirked, lifting our thick bangs into crests.

As the plane came closer to a rank of mountains, the pilot refolded his map and concentrated. He followed several lanes between peaks, weaving past a cluster of thatched huts. I saw a boy run out of one of those little gray domes. He stared at us, looking up from his dirt yard, and I thought about the life he led so far from any road or town. Did he hike to a school each day or simply herd cattle, clucking them down to the rapids a mile away where a yellow surge cascaded over a cliff?

It occurred to me that this boy might have met one of the university students forced by the government to spearhead a rural reeducation program, introducing the principles of Marxism. Who knew? Maybe Yared's girlfriend was somewhere down there. He had shown me a picture of her one morning when we got onto the bus, and he had shaken his head wistfully after I asked where she was, saying he didn't know anymore since she had been reassigned.

And what about the government radio broadcasts? Did that boy on the mountain sit with his father in the evening next to the embers, listening to Radio Ethiopia on a battery-powered radio? Had he heard missionaries described as foreign imperialists who were pacifying Ethiopians, trying to block the progress of the revolution? Had he heard also the lone announcer at the Radio Voice of the Gospel who tried to carefully rebut Marxism without naming it, asking how political change could last if people's hearts had not been changed?

Something silver glimmered off to the left and Nat pointed, tapping Mom and Dad. An airplane was resting in an impossibly small clearing. It was a big plane, a DC-3 judging by its twin engines and fat body. It looked as if it had been set down there completely intact. However, as we flew closer, we saw that the fuselage was cracked.

The pilot shouted, "There's a real botch job. An Ethiopian Airlines plane—ran out of fuel and pancaked."

Another fifteen minutes and the pilot started talking into his radio, changing the ascent of the Cessna, curving around one peak so that we would be pointed at the next. Then I saw what had to be our landing strip: a narrow lane of grass that rose uphill, no wider than twenty yards across and not much longer than a football field.

"You gotta be kidding," I shouted to Nat, whose eyes were gaping.

The pilot swooped the plane into position so that it would match the incline of the mountain. When we touched down, everything skipped and began to bobble. A wing dipped as we crossed a bowl-like depression. Still the pilot did not cut the throttle. In fact, he roared the engine and shouted, "I don't fancy having to get out to push!"

As he topped the rise and turned the plane downhill, the pilot finally cut the engine then shouted, "Righto, can one of you lads jump
out and put that chock under a wheel?"

Seeing the big yellow wedge underneath my seat, I eased open
the door and stepped down. After I had kicked the chock into place,
glancing at the still whirling propeller, I realized we had drawn attention. An eight- or ten-year-old boy was standing on a boulder thirty
yards above us, transfixed despite the fact that his herd of goats was
scrambling away. I also saw a ribbon of red dirt with a man jogging
into view wearing a wool greatcoat and carrying a rifle.

He slowed to a walk, then called out emphatically to my father, who
was climbing from the plane: "Te-NAH-steh-lin. Dehna NEH?"

When he arrived, he shook my father's hand in traditional fashion, gripping himself at the wrist as if offering his hand as a gift. He
shook my own hand, too, and I felt the crust of his calluses, rough as
tree bark.

Dad explained quietly that this was the head of the local gebere
association, and I was surprised. Though his brows pulled together
anxiously, he treated us with great respect, not the brusque insolence I
was accustomed to from the kebeles in Addis.

"In KWAHN deh-na meh TAH," he pronounced, meaning welcome. Then in English, "We have watch HOUSE." And he pointed
back up the path, around the bend toward where the mission station
must be situated.

Our bags were off the plane, and it was time for the pilot to de-
part. I became nervous seeing him climb into the Cessna to start the
engine. I wanted him to walk with us to the station. What if bandits
were waiting—like the ones who attacked the station near the Somali
border? Or what if our two-way radio didn't work anymore and we
had no way to contact mission headquarters?

However, the pilot just called out a quick "Cheerio" and as soon
as Dad handed the yellow chock through the window, he gave the
engine full throttle, trying to reach maximum speed before he got to
the end of the descending runway. Down there, the land fell away at a
drop-off. Instead of the plane leaving the mountain, the mountain left
the plane. In fact, the Cessna sank a bit as it shot off the final lip of
land. It became half-obscured before swooping into view, hanging in

space like a giant kite. Then it passed beyond the next mountain and disappeared, gone except for a slight hum.

I turned toward the rest of my family, afraid of the new quiet, aware that our only companions were a man with a rifle and a goat-herding boy in a dirty smock. Our suitcases were scattered on the short cropped grass of this runway, which doubled as a pasture, judging from the scattered cow patties. I looked at Mom, who must have seen alarm in my eyes because she sighed and smiled sympathetically.

"Toto," she said, "we're not in Kansas anymore."

ere in Iowa, I like to drive in snowstorms, holding the wheel loosely and letting it spin, knowing that to keep any control I must surrender some. I like to walk in ice storms, too, hearing the tree limbs crackle or pop like rifle shots, smashing to the ground with a spray of ice shards. Or to go out onto the ice, stomping to test it, then shuffling toward the central depths, where sometimes a new crack rips away from me and comes back like a sonic boomerang, leaving a white jag of lightning against the blackness between my feet.

I come home to my brick house, where my wife teases me about such risk-taking jaunts, but if I turn on the TV and flip to *American Idol* or a college bowl game, I become inexplicably despondent. I just want to return to the night, careening our van-like car across a snow-covered lawn or taking a polar plunge in a river.

Sunday comes and I show up in the pew for what must now be at least the 2,500th time (based on a steady attendance of at least fifty times a year for fifty years), but I feel inexplicably sleepy down there under the lectern. Even though the epistle reading is a provocative, metaphorical one, I have trouble hanging onto Paul's old, old words, having heard them too many times: "If I speak in the tongues of mortals and of angels but have not love, I am a noisy gong or a clanging cymbal."

I know there is something important for me to hear here—about caring for others, not just myself—but the man at the lectern might as well be a bombulating gong or clashing cymbal. He is so dapper in his polka-dot bowtie, and his voice is perfectly modulated. And what I hear is a kind of *boda-boo, boda-bum, boda-kish-kish-kish.*

Then the deacon comes down the aisle with the glossy gold-bound

Gospel high in the air, and even though this is the most important stuff of all—from the story of Jesus himself—I strain to stay focused on the oft-recited lines, barely able to hear the irony that is inherent in this particular passage, here in the midst of a very familiar community. Jesus has returned to the synagogue of his youth, back in Nazareth, where everyone knows his mother and father, and he is reading from the book of Isaiah, giving them a well-known passage like the one the deacon has given us: "The Spirit of the Lord is on me, because he has anointed me to preach good news to the poor. He has sent me to proclaim freedom for the prisoners and recovery of sight for the blind, to release the oppressed. . . ."

He is behaving as might be expected of a visiting son, back from his travels. But then Jesus does the unthinkable. He announced, "Today this scripture is fulfilled in your hearing."

Here is what happens next in the story. As soon as Jesus sits down, the crowd begins to murmur. He can tell that they are dismissing him because they can't see him as anything other than one of Joseph's sons, perhaps even born out of wedlock. In reaction, he declares, "Truly I tell you, no prophet is accepted in the prophet's hometown." Then, to press his point home, Jesus gives the example of Elijah, who had to go to a foreign widow in Sidon to find food and shelter.

When he is done barbing all the people of his parents' synagogue— his neighborhood church, in effect—they are so incensed that they drag him right to the edge of a cliff, determined to shove him off. This is not a status-quo insurance agent peddling pension plans. He is claiming he has come to free prisoners and to release the oppressed. Yet it is so easy to forget this rabble-rousing reality—to be lulled into sleepy apathy by the sheer repetition of his words.

How I want it all to be different sometimes—to be wildly dangerous and important and worth every risk. To be as remarkably revolutionary as it seemed in the mountains of southern Ethiopia in 1977.

Thirty

After we couldn't hear the plane any longer, we hoisted suitcases to our shoulders and carried them the last mile to our compound, stopping often to catch our breath in the thin air. The gebere leader came along, insisting on carrying a suitcase though he had to counterbalance it against his rifle. When finally we rounded the last bend and I could see down into the little saddle where the station stood, it appeared much the way I remembered: two whitewashed bungalows perched fifty yards from a tin-walled clinic. The slope that fell away beyond the buildings brought back the near-vertigo I had felt as a child—and the amazement of seeing a line of fire wriggling slowly upward.

Mom and Dad pointed out the house that was ours, explaining that the other one might become a home for a nurse. They brought us to our front door and unlocked it, paying the gebere leader a few Ethiopian *birr*. Since they had stayed here only a month, everything was sparse, including the room Nat and I would share: a simple whitewashed box with a four-paned window. I wondered if this could be the same room I had slept in as a four-year-old—where I had wakened to a haze of smoke against the ceiling.

I marveled as I stared out that window. Even though I was a decade older, the place still inspired respectful awe. There was almost too much horizon to bear. On the other side of a little garden, blue sky took over, soaring over a wide expanse of tan savannah. Twenty miles away, across all that openness, stood another range of mountains, deeply shadowed, and beyond that more mountains, glowing with sunlight on one side but almost black on the other.

Here on this wooded ridge, far from the gunshots and checkpoints of Addis, everything seemed wonderfully spacious and free, yet I had become so accustomed to living within boundaries that I was wary and needed time to gather courage for any exploration. The next morning, when the house was still swallowed in clouds, I could see only gray eddies swirling by the windows. Then the mist tore, and I almost lost my balance looking down to a faraway shelf of land, where a farmer in his shawl-like shamma—a speck of brown and cream—was wrestling a tiny wooden plow behind tiny oxen.

I pulled on some jeans and shuffled into the chilly living room to look out our bigger "picture window." I wanted to go out into it all, but I had heard so many stories about missionaries being under siege that I was almost afraid to open the door. Instead, for a while I joined Nat in rifling through cabinets and shelves, taking inventory of the personal possessions left by the last family. There were action novels like *Where Eagles Dare* by Alistair MacLean, board games like *Snakes and Ladders*, and a battery-powered phonograph with a set of albums.

The two of us spent thirty minutes just feeding old albums into that box-like record player, holding imaginary mics to our mouths. We joined the Supremes in singing "Stop in the Name of Love," imitating the scratchy falsetto of their voices. Then we pulled out an even more dated album with a photo of Julie Andrews skipping across an Alpine meadow, guitar case in hand. There was a symphonic buildup before her exuberant voice burst forth, celebrating the flower-studded mountain slopes and their special drawn-out "muuuuusic." And as we lip-synched along, mouthing the lingering words, we faced the picture window and gestured toward all that rugged horizon.

Attracted by the familiar tune, Mom came in from the kitchen, where she had been cooking eggs. She stood with us, patting her chest, happy to have us home again, yet overcome by the emotions that Andrews's soaring voice unlocked. Years ago, we had all gone as a family to see *The Sound of Music* in Kansas City. It was just after we moved back to the United States—when we were still trying to recover from the last stint in Ethiopia—and Mom remembered now how my brother Johnathan had been so transported that he begged to go right back into the theater and watch again. She felt sorry that she and Dad had not let him watch a second time—to enjoy the release of that other war-threatened family escaping over the Alps.

Aware of Johnathan's absence, I realized I was becoming by default the "oldest brother." Whereas he had always been a natural leader, happy to plan and prompt, I had tended to stand back critiquing. I felt the weight of my new role as I looked to my younger brother. When breakfast was over, I pushed myself to be proactive, asking, "Wanna go out with slingshots?"

Nat nodded, so I led the way to our suitcases, unpacking my Y-shaped weapon and the other one that Dave Iwan had helped Nat to make just before the holiday. Armed, we stepped out a side door like cats prowling unfamiliar territory. We were afraid to venture far, so we tiptoed down the backyard into the garden, where we had seen a large African kite swooping toward a lemon tree, and as we approached, we were thrilled to find not just one of these hawk-like birds, but four or five gathered round a compost pit, picking at scraps.

Nat and I raised our slingshots slowly, pulling back the leather pouches, and when the kites startled into the air, we let loose, missing narrowly. We reloaded as quickly as we could, trying to hit them as they went into a tight swirling circle. Again and again, we missed, amazed at how the large birds made a game of each of our projectiles, back-flapping or dropping a wing with an agility that seemed impossibly quick.

The kites finally dispersed, and we galloped after one that had flown over our house. It glided toward a row of eucalyptus trees a little farther up the incline, only to swerve when several large, hook-billed birds rose on tiptoe, flapping a warning. We, on the other hand, crept closer, realizing we might have an even more interesting target! Ibises.

Silently, we slinked up to that line of eucalyptuses, where a thorn fence screened the compound of a nearby Ethiopian family. Then we took aim. I was hesitant due to opposing emotions: excitement about getting close to such exotic creatures, guilt about trying to hit them, and nervousness about being near the house of people who might not want us firing rocks over their thatched roof. Although Bulki seemed wonderfully removed from the tensions of the revolution (nothing like the closely surrounded compound of Bingham Academy), I was experienced enough to know that the residents here might still be affected.

Yet I was having too much fun with my slingshot to simply walk away. When I saw that my first rock caught in the leafy cover and fell back harmlessly, I shot again. Nat did too. We both fired away at the nervous but stubborn birds until, at last, a ricocheting rock penetrated the canopy and we heard a startled squawk.

As one of the big black-and-white ibises flapped out of the tree, calling an indignant "Char-lee," Nat and I grinned. We were startled then by an unexpected outburst of giggling. I peered through a gap in the thorn fence and spotted two young boys standing beside the door of their mud-walled *tukel*. When we waved, they walked toward us, slipping through the gap while speaking their local tongue, Gofa. Unlike the brash antagonists at the Bingham fence, they were not shouting aggravating questions or mimicking our actions. On the other hand, they weren't saying much we could understand. We could only shake our heads and try sign language.

The older one, roughly ten, gestured to my slingshot, wanting a turn, so I handed it to him. He was shaved except for a topknot of hair, and he had scrawny arms. He held the stick in the wrong hand, against his chest. He reversed it after I showed him, but he pulled back the pouch so weakly that the rock sailed only fifteen feet, not unlike the way I had shot the slingshot on my first attempt. Satisfied, he handed back the contraption, smiling shyly, glad to have just tried the thing.

Having gotten through this first interaction with someone local, Nat and I grew more confident as the day unfolded. When Mom called us in for lunch and asked if we would go get Dad, I didn't balk. I tried to be more like Johnathan had been with me in Troy. "C'mon, bro," I said, "I'll race you."

Down the slope, the two of us thundered, sprinting right to the door of the clinic, where we were met by a startled cluster of patients and family members who stood from their benches. We did what we could to be properly courteous, bowing and saying the only greeting we knew, "Tenahstehlin." Although this was an Amharic greeting, not Gofa, it seemed to engender a warm response. People smiled and rose to shake hands. Then I noticed that several of the sickest people didn't have energy to respond. There was a shivering man with smoky eyes and shallow breaths, perhaps suffering from malaria. There was a weary woman with a tire-like goiter around her neck, signaling a lack of iodine. And an old man got up from his bench very feebly, bowing from where he stood, not able to take a step.

Dad was busy taking each of them, one at a time, into his examining room, where a locally trained dresser assisted and offered translation. When we joined them in the examining room, it was hard not to stare at this assistant since he was a recovered leper and had lost most of his eyebrows plus the tips of several fingers. However, he took away any self-consciousness by asking Nat and me questions in careful English before going back to work quizzing the lame man, who apparently had an infected foot. We watched as he bathed the pus-filled wound with alcohol then lanced it with a scalpel. We watched as he applied antibiotic ointment and gauze. And it was all so interesting that, after lunch, the two of us decided we would like to go back again and spend the rest of the afternoon.

We returned to help Joseph, the dresser, as he bottled pills in the closet-like dispensary. It felt good to be doing something as practical as scooping penicillin capsules out of a metal tray, counting them one by one as they dribbled through a funnel into glass bottles. While adding cotton and screwing the caps on, I reveled at the strange blend of medicinal odors: bitter powder, sharp antiseptic, unguent oil. I also reveled at the slow-but-successful attempt to communicate with Joseph using a mishmash of English and Amharic and pantomimes.

This soft-spoken, eager dresser taught Nat and me a number of words in the Gofa language as the afternoon went by—such as *yelis* for "father" and *nagha* for "son"—and I felt pleased to be making headway culturally. After we closed up the clinic, I felt confident enough to go somewhere completely by myself. I slipped out the kitchen door without Nat and hiked the little peak that rose behind the bowl-like saddle of our station. At the top I could stand higher than any part of the mountain. While the sun set, lifting a gray shawl over the shoulders of the low rises, I felt the wind yank at me, making me sway. It lifted my hair and blew in my ears. It ruffled my shirt and pants. I just stood there, looking out over this realm that could be a potential home, and I realized I had not been alone like this since leaving Troy—completely alone in the pleasant way I had known when hiking the woods near the Missouri River.

For nearly three months now, whether I was at the youth hostel or at Good Shepherd, I had been inside fences and surrounded by people. If I drifted into the forested area behind my dorm, there was always some younger child nearby. Even if I went to the bathroom, there was likely to be another guy in the next stall.

I held my arms out in the glorious wind. Like the lone kite that sailed by on an updraft, I wanted to glide right out into this open, limitless realm. I called out softly, celebrating my new liberty—not loud enough of course to bring the two Ethiopian boys out of their thatched house, where smoke was rising from the evening fire. Just loud enough to alert God.

"Yes," I murmured, sending my voice into the wind, and though I couldn't hear any physical response, it seemed to me as if God might be calling back, "Yes, indeed!"

Thirty-One

Geographers define the word "place" as a "meaningful space," arguing that each place is created by those who bring it into being, assigning meaning. Until a time of intervention, there is no place, just space, which is something you pass through. Place, by contrast, is a pause in the movement, a stopping, an attentive staying, and out of that pause comes the necessary meaning to define or claim. "Here," the new arrival says, "this is my retreat, my eagle's nest, this mountaintop in southern Ethiopia."

Meaningful in what sense, though? A randomly viewed landscape might be so meaningful that it is remembered for a lifetime; however, it is still seen at a remove—not like a home, which is seen from inside. And what happens when someone, after seeing a landscape from outside, wants to enter it and create a home? Suddenly this new person brings a meaning to the space that collides with all the old meanings. In fact, if the new person wields enough power or influence, the old meanings may get shoved aside. What was this mountaintop before I arrived with my parents, moving into an adobe bungalow built by foreigners? What stories were attached to this high saddle of land with its swathe of eucalyptus trees? What was its essential meaning, and to whom?

In the early 1800s, after a century and a half of passing Africa and rarely stopping, the European colonial forces began to look inward, into the interior, and started making the first incremental steps into that vast landscape. Prior to that, they barely held a toehold on the coast, in places such as the Cape Coast Fort, defined by commodities like slaves and gold, or the Dutch-built Cape Town on the southern tip of Africa, where ships could drop anchor to resupply from local farms while sailors recuperated in a two-hundred-bed hospital and carpenters repaired hulls.

These tiny coastal places had a purely commercial meaning, existing to help European merchants exchange manufactured goods (like knives or axe heads) for slaves or ivory, palm oil or raw gold. For them, Africa was a source of raw materials, not much more. And from the vantage point of the trading posts, the rest of the continental landscape seemed to promise simply more of the same: immense resources.

The spaces the Europeans saw seemed virtually empty, ready for occupation. Or if they were occupied, they seemed occupied by poorly organized, misguided people who had not given proper definition to the space, having no apparent sense of purpose. These colonial front-runners did not see, in most cases, the elaborate social structures that already gave significance to everything, such as the age-based hierarchy of agricultural achievement among the Igbo clan that Chinua Achebe memorialized—or the way that the ancestral guides, or *Egwugwu*, assigned spiritual power to certain trees and streams. These long-established structures of meaning, despite having helped to define southeastern Nigeria for centuries, were pushed aside as powerful intruders assigned other meanings to the space, employing a new educational system to support their meanings, and a new religion as well.

In Ethiopia, too, the incoming missionaries denied local meanings that had been assigned to the land, disregarding the notion that certain trees and hills were sacred sites where sacrifices should be offered. New converts refused to leave a portion of a slaughtered goat as an offering to the spirits, parting ways with their own families over that long-kept tradition. They refused to acknowledge the old meanings, replacing them with new ones.

It sounds all wrong, put this way. Completely blind and arrogant. But don't we all do some form of this regularly? When we buy a house, wherever it might be, don't we bring our views with us, assigning new meanings that redefine the space, and hanging our own quirky icons where others used to hang? For instance, as I sit here on my white leather couch in a 1930s brick house under a tapestry my grandmother made—of a medieval hunter with his hawk—do I not supplant the meanings that used to be given to this place by an elderly woman who loved cats and, according to all accounts, ignored the yard altogether, allowing grass to grow two feet high? And didn't she supplant the meanings given by a doctor before her, who loved horticulture and grew elderberries and banks of iris? Didn't he, also, supplant the golfers who used to chip balls right over this knoll when it was part of a turn-of-the-century country club? And what about the farmer before that? Or the Mesquaki woman who may have tried to find morel mushrooms here or to trade maple syrup?

What has happened to the meanings those people used to give to this same fifty-by-two-hundred-foot strip of space? And why does my sense of place matter more than theirs? Or does it really? Is this space itself the only thing that really lasts in the end, carrying with it all the history that has been inscribed, eventually dragging down the doctor's leftover elderberry bush, not to mention the renegade antique golf ball or, deeper still, the flint arrowhead that went awry three hundred years ago, never to be found again?

And is all this absorbed history—this subtle record of small imperial urges—the reason that new occupants often turn back later to use the names of those who were pushed aside? Kingman Boulevard, in honor of the farmer who used to till this hill. And farther to the south, in the countryside below this city, a row of towns named Keokuk, Oskaloosa, Ottumwa, whose ghostly names remain like a badge of quiet penance on the breast of the invader.

We could stay home, I suppose, and build high walls, trying to let others have their own realms. But what a lonely world that would be—full of castaways on static, never-changing islands.

Or perhaps we could cross the borders, doing it as humbly as possible, attuned to every meaning that might already exist, trying to encounter the landscape as an already defined place. We could try to see through the eyes of one who is already there, staying as receptive as possible, given the powerful compulsions of our beliefs, our desires, our hope to make it home.

Thirty-Two

Since Mom and Dad were still trying to concentrate on Nat and me, we all remained at home that first Sunday to have our own church service. This was Palm Sunday, so we discussed the gospel account of Jesus riding a donkey into Jerusalem with crowds throwing down palm branches. Dad said that the Jewish people wanted Jesus to bring political change, rescuing them from the tyranny of the Romans. They did not realize God's changes start internally. Soul first, then body.

Like any teenage son, I listened with a mix of respect and resistance. Even though I had seen the damage of the Marxist revolution, I wondered how people would ever get physically free if they were focused only on spiritual matters. And what should Christians do when a political system went bad? Just pray?

The next Sunday, Easter Sunday, my parents decided it was time for us to get out and attend a local church. I felt nervous, but I tried to be upbeat. It had rained, so everything was dripping as we hiked along the ridge. Beside the farm plots, banana leaves hung down broad as elephant ears, and I entertained myself by tugging a few of these leaves, dumping streamlets on my unsuspecting brother.

The church turned out to be just another round, thatch-roofed structure like most family tukels, only larger. Inside, I couldn't see, but I could hear everyone murmuring in Gofa. Then my eyes adjusted, helped by the threads of light that pricked down through the thatch, and I made out about twenty men seated on split logs with shammas around their shoulders, clustered across from an equal number of women seated on woven mats wearing thick blue cotton dresses and covering their heads with gauzy nettas.

The sermon was all in Gofa, therefore impossible to follow except when I picked up bits of the sketchy translation offered by Joseph, the clinic dresser, who had arrived just in time to help. What struck me was how the congregation started to shout as the minister described the resurrected Jesus appearing to Peter in his fishing boat on Lake Galilee. "He is risen," everyone called out, including the dresser as he translated.

The minister went quiet, and Joseph murmured, "Initsully," accidentally translating into Amharic instead of English. No matter. I remembered this expression. It meant "Let us pray." What followed was much more dynamic than any praying I had done in the last six years back at the First Baptist Church in Troy, Kansas. All the men got down off the split logs, joining the women on the floor. They knelt and leaned forward until their foreheads touched the woven mats of banana fiber. Then they all called out in a jumble of individual prayers, whispering urgent requests or blurting thanks.

As I bowed in the middle of this hive of buzzing prayer, I had no hesitation about joining in, speaking quiet English: "Thanks for bringing us to this place in the mountains. Please keep Nancy safe at Gambela. Keep Johnathan safe, too." I felt strangely linked to everyone around me, part of a unified song as I went on, "And Lord, thank you for these people who have welcomed us."

I was overwhelmed for a moment by the simple fact that we had all come together in trust, not as enemies divided by opposing worldviews, not as communists and capitalists or locals and foreigners. It was a wonderful relief to simply be accepted.

A few days later, I was still conscious of this warm treatment when one of the elders from that rural church showed up at our house. I galloped down to the clinic to fetch Dad, and after he returned with me, I stayed in the living room listening as he spoke with the visitor in halting Amharic and Gofa. I even helped my mother serve tea.

This elder was a white-haired, soft-spoken man with sunken cheeks and a furrowed brow. At one point he set down his teacup very carefully so that he could lift an old notebook from our bookshelf and kiss the cover—a black-and-white photo of former Emperor Selassie. We did not even know this notebook existed—an apparent holdover from the last missionary family—or we would have hidden it. Photos of the emperor were illegal now. It was even illegal to use old currency that featured his portrait, which had been replaced by bills and coins that featured "progressive" images such as an Ethiopian scientist at a microscope.

Moved by this act of loyalty, Dad tried to ask the older man how things were going for the church under the new government, but he only shook his head, not comfortable voicing what he was thinking. He turned instead to his reason for visiting: a request for Bibles. Even Amharic ones would do, he explained, since children were now studying in Amharic and it was the trade language of the region. They would be glad even for a few New Testaments.

My father replied that he would try to get some from the printing press in Addis, but it might take a while. Then the old man nodded deeply, clasping his hands in front of him and shaking them up and down. Anyone else, chancing on the scene, might have thought Dad had just cured him of cancer.

Another day or two passed and we got confirmation from Missionary Aviation Fellowship that a pilot would be arriving to fly Nat and me to Addis, taking Mom and Dad along so they could restock supplies. I did not expect to feel so disappointed. I missed Nancy of course, but otherwise I felt content to stay at Bulki for much longer than the two and a half weeks that had passed.

Then on the morning when we were scheduled to leave—a Saturday—the radio operator in Addis Ababa explained that our MAF pilot was stranded at a station to the east, waiting for another plane to bring him a part for a minor repair. He still hoped to pick us up as he returned to Addis, but he would be delayed an extra day, if not longer.

"Fine," said Dad, "we can go to church tomorrow down in the valley."

Mom raised an eyebrow: "If he gets the plane fixed, he could show up!"

"On the Sabbath? The week after Easter?"

"Well, maybe!" Mom interjected.

"Yeah, Dad," added Nat. "Somebody should stay at the house."

"Good idea," he said. "You two can stay while Tim and I go. And we can hike back before noon, just in case."

Although I wondered about ducking out when this flight could arrive, I felt emboldened by Dad's attitude. Besides, his protest made sense to me—"Even if they do come, they won't arrive before noon. They'll go to church. They're missionaries!" So I left the house with him the next morning at 7:30, intrigued to take a look at life down in the dry, hot valley, closer to where the Bodi and Mursi people lived, those fierce clans who required young men to prove themselves by killing an enemy.

The hike was long but not strenuous, since we were going down the mountain taking switchbacks at a near jog. "Coming back's not going to be as easy," I pointed out, but Dad dismissed my caution with his standard retort: "No problem!"

When we finally reached the church, it seemed quite different than the prayer house on the mountain, not just because it was out in the savannah surrounded by tall dry grasses, but because it was square instead of round, and tin-roofed instead of thatched. I was a bit disappointed actually to find everything more modern and familiar. I suppose I had expected, with all the talk of primitive tribes in the valleys, to find a ragged lean-to surrounded by a wall of acacia thorns.

Since this was communion Sunday, an usher came around with a basket of large bread crumbs then an aluminum tray of tiny glasses like we had used in Troy, Kansas—completely familiar except that the liquid was not the purple of Welch's grape juice; it was yellow like apple juice.

"What's in the glasses?" I whispered.

"Honey water," Dad murmured.

"Like tej?"

"No, it's not alcoholic. You'll be fine."

"But what about parasites?"

"Just pray, then drink."

I knew he was half-joking, but I did pray before I drank. The liquid tasted sweet as sugar cane, although it had the sour aftertaste of clover and ferment. I swallowed, then prayed again, "Lord, no amoeba, please," which seemed absurd right after drinking the most sacred symbol for Christ.

Out here in a valley that could be reached only by walking or riding a mule, the glass thimble-cups and the precise disc-like tray with its punched-out holes seemed almost surreal. Here in a mud-walled church hundreds of kilometers from Addis Ababa, the tray was so alien—so incredibly different than customary clay pots or drinking gourds—that I felt as if I was staring at a UFO. The gadget even looked like a UFO as it hovered from hand to hand.

I fought back a wave of amusement as members of the Ethiopian congregation reached for this "flying saucer." Each adult took a tiny cup with thick, calloused fingers, concentrating closely, eyes closed, before tipping the liquid back to flow through parted lips. Even though I felt amused, I also felt a profound sense of blessedness as I watched them lower their heads in silent contemplation. I felt thankful just for getting to share this tiny drink.

As soon as the service was over, the elders gathered around Dad, eager to hear news from the mission. They made it clear they wanted to include me through the help of a teenager who knew some English. I appreciated their kindness and tried to answer as graciously as possible. When they asked, "How about it, do you like Ethiopian food?" I said, "Absolutely. It is the best food in the world."

They laughed.

I didn't know Gofa, but I could at least use a few words from the national language. "Betam itafitel," I said, remembering the Amharic phrase for "Very tasty."

"Aha," they said, "Amrinya tifelagalow." Or "He speaks Amharic." Then they added, "So you must stay and eat with us."

Dad shook his head and pointed up the mountain, explaining that a plane might be coming.

"A little time only," they replied. "Tenish, tenish."

What could we say? We did not want to offend them. Besides, we loved eating *injera ba wat.* So we followed the five or six older men across the dirt yard to the minister's house, stepping inside the thatched interior to greet his wife, who stood up from where she had been fanning a cooking fire.

As this hostess brought carved stools for us to sit on, I briefly teased Dad about our noon deadline.

"We'll walk fast," he said.

"You mean run?"

The minister's wife squatted over the fire circle, pouring batter and

watching closely as it spread in a bubbly pancake on her clay grid-
dle. Then the oldest daughter, who looked close to my age, came by,
not meeting my eyes or saying a word as she placed a basin on the
ground to catch the water she poured over my hands. She had her
hair wrapped in a tight blue turban like most women, which gave
her an elegant forehead and accentuated her somber eyes. She was a
pretty girl with a serious face, and I felt weird getting this servant-like
treatment knowing that, if we were in America or even Addis Ababa,
she would be sitting right with us, eating and talking. How would she
behave if she went to school with me at Good Shepherd? Like my
rowdy Ethiopian classmate Lydia, who was forever being asked by
our biology teacher to put down the beaker of acetone or to refrain
from giggling?

After a few more formalities and the passing of a tray with parched
grain, the main course began to arrive, served on a big tin platter that
rested neatly atop a round table of woven straw. The main dish was
doro wat, poured onto crepe-like *injera*. I broke off bits of these crepes
and used them to pinch morsels of the stew, pulling meat off a drum-
stick or breaking into a boiled egg. The warm red *wat* was rich with
pepper and onion. It was so spicy that even the minister began to
shrug the sweat from his forehead.

When I finally sat back to breathe, the Ethiopian men chuckled
at my flushed face, which caused the minister to call to his daughter. Wordless, she fetched a bottle of Orange Fanta from a crate near
the door—a perfect antidote for all the spices. After I thanked her, I
cooled my mouth with the sugary liquid, then lit back into the meal,
working on a milder stew, a chickpea puree called *misir wat*. Everyone
was feeling full and satisfied now, and ready to talk, so the minister
and the other men began telling a story about a missionary who came
to the area years ago and encountered a lion while hiking between
villages. They got great pleasure out of describing him dashing to the
top of a hill, banging a pot to scare away the predator.

This story led to others, and soon they were describing, with vig-
orous gestures, a time of persecution by the local Orthodox priests,
who had rounded up all the Protestant evangelists and ministers and
jailed them. Only one evangelist had eluded the search parties, yet he
bravely led a group of wives and friends to the jail, delivering food
right in front of the unsuspecting guards.

"Was this before all the recent troubles?" Dad asked.

"Awo," they murmured.

"Back in the time of Selassie?"

"Awo."

"And what was the reason given for the jailings?"

They clucked and one of the oldest men, a wrinkled fellow with smoky eyes, tried to explain, his words being translated by the teenage boy at my side.

"He says," the boy explained, "that the governor did not like having a new religion since the people would not obey. He says the priests were angry we did not pay the priest tax. So they burnt prayer houses and beat people. Can you believe it? They killed three of the old ones."

All this talk about the past had made Dad curious. He wanted to know how long ago this particular church was founded, and who the first members were, which somehow led the minister to describe a local boy who was captured by northern slave traders a few years before World War II. Apparently, this boy had escaped from his Amhara master, returning all the way across the Blue Nile and hundreds of miles of mountains, only to be recaptured. As the minister described the distress of the boy's family, who had lost him not once but twice, I thought that I heard a distant hum. I concentrated and heard it again—a monotone whine, almost like a flair of tinnitus—so I broke in suddenly.

"Dad, did you hear that?"

He frowned. "What?"

"It sounded like an airplane."

He shook his head. "Not on Sunday."

I knew he was hampered by terrible hearing, but I could see that the minister was waiting, looking from him to me and back again, so I made no further protest. I stayed silent as the minister told the rest of the story, describing how the local villagers gathered a small fortune in goats and grain then convinced an Amhara landlord to chase down the slave traders and buy the boy back.

It was an inspiring story—the sort that caused goose bumps. "Egzhiaber yemeskin," my father said, giving praise to God. He seemed delighted by the way this story illustrated the biblical concept of redemption. I, on the other hand, was intrigued that a person could be forced into slavery only forty years ago, right here where we sat. I was intrigued, too, that here in the Bulki area the first Protestant converts had been a liberating force. After all, hadn't the new form of Christianity helped to break through the ancient tribal and Orthodox hierarchy that separated poor from rich? Hadn't many of the new Christians become educated, progressing as teachers and pharmacists and local leaders instead of staying trapped in perpetual servitude?

We had to go. After offering extended thanks to the minister, and to his wife and daughter (who covered their mouths to hide smiles), we started up the mountain, striding quickly. It was tough going because the day had become hot and the injera was heavy in our stomachs, but we kept walking fast, not even stopping to rest as the surrounding ground became greener, broken by patches of wooded shade.

We were only a mile from the station when I heard what I had been afraid to hear all along—the same high whine of an engine that I had heard in the valley, only more intense. Dad heard it, too, and began to jog. I sprinted away, hoping I could intercept the plane.

Was it landing or taking off? That was my question, and I had a sinking feeling because the sound rose in pitch as I got closer.

Suddenly a single-engine Cessna shot out from behind the slope in front of me, no longer muffled by the mountain.

"Nooo," I shouted, waving my arms and leaping. But the plane arced right over me and roared past my father. Then it swung to the north and climbed toward cruising altitude.

We ran for the house, now only half a mile away, but it was locked and a note was pinned to the door: "Have to go. Pilot can't wait. Says he will come back in a few days. Key is under mat. Love, Mom."

I pounded on the door as Dad looked for the key. "We shouldn't have gone down there. It was a stupid idea," I shouted.

I was scared. I was again aware that we were living out here on the edge of nowhere. Would that plane really return? Were Mom and Nat going to be okay separate from us?

For a second I recalled the DC-3 pancaked against the side of a mountain north of Bulki, which gave me a chill. How would we even know whether Mom and Nat had gotten back safely, since my father never did the communicating on the radio and might not know how to operate it? And what about Nancy? Would I ever see her again?

"Think of it as an adventure," Dad said, trying to take some of the edge off my panic.

I tried to look less upset; however, I was not relieved. I felt, once again, the incredible fragility of the way we lived out here on the edge of Ethiopian civilization, where evangelists had been jailed for what they believed, where churches had been burnt to the ground, where people still remembered a boy kidnapped twice and dragged off into slavery.

Thirty-Three

One has to wonder—that is, after moving from the middle of the United States to a remote mountaintop in southern Ethiopia—whether one really belongs. And that is a problem compounded by the way the United States has flexed its muscles internationally.

All the way back when I was a student at Wheaton College, bastion of conservative American evangelicalism, the Republican candidate Ronald Reagan came to drum up votes for his run against President Carter, himself an openly born-again president. Reagan talked the right biblical talk, lauding us for heeding Jesus's injunction, "Go ye, therefore, and teach all nations." He held our college up as a true American model, a beacon on a hill, implying that we should take our light out there into the world and illuminate every corner. And afterward he got a huge ovation as he was presented with a stuffed Perry Mastodon, the cuddly mascot adopted by Wheaton College after a fossilized mastodon was discovered on the grounds of the campus.

Being a nineteen-year-old son of missionaries, I didn't know what exactly to think about Ronald Reagan, except that he seemed a bit too warm and folksy. But I was disturbed a year later, after he had won the election, to read editorials in our school paper criticizing him for his backing of Spanish-speaking dictators who claimed to be anticommunist allies. I became particularly upset when I learned that the United States had been linked to the assassination of one of the most outspoken Catholic leaders in Central America—the archbishop of El Salvador, Oscar Romero.

All of this was happening during the post-Vietnam era of the Cold War, and Reagan, blocked by a cautious Congress, was trying to even old scores by running a shadowy communist resistance through the

CIA. His hidden campaign involved, among other things, mining a harbor in Nicaragua and funding a guerrilla army by, strange as it may seem, selling weapons to Iran with the help of Israel. And at the heart of this anti-communist crusade was the training facility called "School of the Americas," which would soon be transferred out of Panama into Fort Benning, Georgia, because of the out-of-control behavior of one of the school's own graduates, Col. Manuel Noriega.

In any case, our School of the Americas' support for pro-America leaders like Noriega included training for military death squads in the nation of El Salvador, who were paid to target any government resisters no matter how peaceful their approach. According to the ruling junta in El Salvador, all these resisters were communists who had to be wiped out. The slaughter was so indiscriminate that Archbishop Romero finally issued an appeal directly to the armed forces: "We are your people. The peasants you kill are your own brothers and sisters. When you hear the voice of the man commanding you to kill, remember instead the voice of God: Thou Shalt Not Kill. . . . No soldier is obliged to obey an order contrary to the law of God." Ironically, it was the very next day, as he was lifting a chalice in a hospital chapel, that Romero himself was gunned down.

That was the sort of stuff I was learning about one summer when I came back from college to our new home in Kansas and claimed to my father that maybe our foreign policy was actually creating communists rather than stopping them. I pushed further, insisting that we were so quick to target potential enemies that legitimate reformers had no chance to define themselves, forced into aligning with capitalism or communism. But my father was having none of it, thinking still of the horrible damages he had seen in Ethiopia. He felt the threat of communism so viscerally that other concerns paled next to it, even if they were life and death. His eyes flashed, and I fell silent while pondering whether maybe, if we would just stay out of other countries altogether, everything would be better. What if Americans just pulled back inside their borders? Would the whole world improve?

Gripped by this new shame, I became embarrassed about my role—and the role of my parents—in exporting American culture.

How gauche of us. Of course we had been wrong to go into Ethiopia. We were as out of place as that aluminum communion tray that was passed around the savannah church below Bulki, a symbol of a whole set of imposed foreign notions.

In fact, I began writing this memoir—what you are reading now— feeling a need to apologize for my appalling ethnocentrism and that of my missionary clan. What right did we have, after all, to impose our ways on a more natural, vulnerable, even innocent society?

Except that, as I worked on the book, recalling the Ethiopia I had encountered as a youth, I began to ask whether that society was truly innocent in the idealized primitive sense that some people imagine when bristling about Western missionaries. In reality, the people of Ethiopia have never been an equivalent to Rousseau's romanticized "savages." They are quite sophisticated—with ancient customs, a carefully observed hierarchy, and a written language that predates our own, going all the way back to the fifth century BC.

Nor are they automatically "noble" in Rousseau's elevated sense. Even today in Ethiopia, the larger tribal groups treat some of the smaller groups as if they are only a step up from indentured servitude. For that matter, in many areas women have few rights. Preadolescent girls may be forced into female circumcision even though it will take away sexual pleasure and cause life-threatening consequences during childbirth. Some are kidnapped and forced into marriage.

These observed flaws may simply help to prove that no culture, whether "developed" or "underdeveloped," is actually sacrosanct in a primal Eden-like way. Which makes me wonder whether there is anything intrinsically wrong with the attempt to promote reform, even if the attempt comes from outside. In Ethiopia, for example, was the missionaries' attempt to treat all humans with equal dignity wrong even though it went against the long-respected hierarchy of Ethiopian culture, the same hierarchy that allowed for slavery? And if that new Protestant equality shook up the traditional gender roles in Ethiopian society, where girls were routinely circumcised as adolescents and forced into early marriage, was that wrong? If that new outlook caused sharecroppers, after centuries of forced deference, to see themselves as equals in the eyes of God with those who had lorded it over them—to even begin to imagine owning their own land—was that wrong? To go a step further, what would Marx have thought?

Some critics would toss the missionary out with the emperor, both of them relegated to the trash heap of history. But let's be fair. If the missionary, then why not the foreign aid worker and the expatriate entrepreneur? And what makes the Chinese consultant any more trustworthy?

The real problem is this, I think: sometimes even the most benevolent soul can harbor superiority.

"They aren't doing things the right way," the well-intentioned, well-educated foreigner begins to think, when really what is meant, down there in the basement of the soul, is this: "They aren't doing things my way."

Thirty-Four

The next morning, thankfully, my father succeeded in getting the radio to work, and found the right frequency. I helped to listen since he had bad hearing. Mom and Nat had arrived. We could expect our own flight in a little over forty-eight hours. We would not be flying all the way to Addis, though. We would have to continue by bus from Jimma.

The radio operator had a scolding tone: "Be at the airstrip at 8:00 a.m. promptly. No delays this time!"

After Dad went down to the clinic, I wandered the house, using up the batteries in the phonograph as I listened to the same Supremes album three or four times. Then I tried to generate some interest in a dog-eared copy of *The Cross and the Switchblade*, a kind of gonzo Christian autobiography that only added to my jumpiness. This violent action story featured street warfare in Brooklyn and a dangerously evangelistic minister who was always on the verge of getting stabbed to death. It didn't help that the gang he was trying to reach—an all Puerto Rican gang—went by the name "Mau Mau" in emulation of rebels who had terrorized the British out of Kenya, a hundred kilometers south of us.

Dad joined me in the middle of the day to eat some sandwiches I had slapped together from a dry loaf and a can of sardines. Then at supper time, I realized he expected me to cook again, so I scrounged in the cupboards until I found a can of beans and a recipe for cornbread. He was amazed that I succeeded with the cornbread, since it had to be baked in the woodstove. As we played chess by lamplight, he kept commenting on how good this bread was, eating his way slowly across the pan.

I moved pawns into the open, creating lanes for my castles. Although I still felt twinges of anxiety, I knew that we were okay for now, and I allowed myself to relax, enjoying the company of my father. He wanted to hear how I felt about school and what Nancy was like. He also wanted a report on how Nat seemed to be doing.

"So do you check on him?" he asked, not expecting to hear that we were meeting for a weekly Bible study. I could tell he was pleased, and I felt once more a sense of my new status in the family—the big brother, the protector.

"What about Johnathan?" I asked, trying to match Dad's family focus. "Have you and Mom heard anything from him?"

I was sobered to learn that my older brother was still struggling with something mysterious that my father wouldn't come right out and explain. Johnathan had gone to see a doctor—that's all that was clear—and when I asked what his symptoms were, Dad hedged: "The main thing is that the tests came out negative, which is what he needed to hear. He's not worrying as much."

Worrying? About what? And why?

I had never thought of Johnathan as a worrier—not like me. He had always been the most competent of the three of us, the most sure of his plans. I could tell my father was concerned, too, even though he was trying to act positive, and this made him appear vulnerable. It was my turn to move, and I saw that Dad's bishop was in danger. If I took it with my castle, I could put his king in check. He seemed distracted, though, and I didn't have the heart to end the game. I took a pawn instead, at which point he surprised me by reversing the whole scenario, taking my castle with a knight and pinning my king.

There was only one other event of importance that happened before our departure to Addis, and it occurred during our second day of waiting. Before Dad went down to the clinic, I told him that the water from our cistern seemed to taste odd. It seemed rancid to me, like old butter.

Dad thought I just didn't like the metallic taste that came from the sheet-metal cistern, which collected water off the roof. He thought also that the taste might come from over-boiling the water. I wasn't convinced, so I went out to the big elevated tank after he left, and climbed up the iron scaffolding to take a look. When I opened the lid and let it bang down against the side of the tank, all I noticed were concentric circles that quivered in the dark pool. Then I saw in one corner what had caused the taste: a small balloon of matted fur—a dead rat.

I shoveled this bloated ball of flesh out of the cistern, which left an oily film on the water, shimmering in ghostly violet. Then I ran down to the clinic to tell Dad, "We've got to drain the tank right away."

He surprised me: "If we empty it, where are we going to get water to refill it?"

Rains were not guaranteed over the next month, even though we were getting closer to the rainy season. He pointed out, too, that the stream where our house worker got gardening water was full of sediment and bacteria. Since none of us had become sick these last few days, he reasoned that we should just boil the water more thoroughly, keeping it on the stove longer.

That night after I had boiled a kettle so long that half of it evaporated, I added several spoonfuls of powdered Tang. Then I fought back my gag reflex and swallowed a mouthful of the hot orange beverage. The problem was that I kept seeing bloated skin and matted fur. After another swallow I gave up altogether and concentrated on the chess game. I was quite willing to skip breakfast in the morning and walk out to the airstrip at dawn, where we sat patiently, remembering the scolding we had received on the radio.

Sure enough, after the plane rolled to a stop, we got an earful from the pilot. "I'm surprised you're here, lads. Figured you'd be taking a hike." However, he let it go after that, and went to work weighing our bags from a scale he hung under the wing. "You'll see I've got a passenger already—an evangelist going to Jimma—plus three crates of IV fluid and a wheelchair. Should be an interesting takeoff."

It was interesting indeed. Even with the engine ratcheted up and the plane vibrating from stem to stern, we dropped heavily as we came off the end of the downhill strip. I clenched the arms of my seat, expecting a jolt. Dad looked pale until the wings caught air and we swooped away. Then he grinned, and the Ethiopian evangelist tried to smile too, looking like he might faint.

This man had probably never flown in an airplane before that morning. He was a wiry, trim fellow in a neat brown suit jacket. But he kept staring out the window wide-eyed, too anxious to answer my father's questions. When we had climbed over the last ridge of mountains and started a steep descent into the Jimma valley, the plane bucked on the surging updrafts. The Ethiopian evangelist went gray. Before I could point to the paper bag in his seat pocket, he leaned over and barfed into the pocket of his carefully pressed suit jacket.

Immediately the plane filled with the stench of his bile, and I felt my own gorge rising, acrid at the back of my throat, like when I had tried to drink some of the boiled dead-rat water. We touched down just in time, and I was able to unlatch a door, stepping into the blessed wind. The pilot, strict about checking instruments, had to wait longer and came out frowning. He shook his head when he looked at us. "Righto, lads," he said, "the worst is over. Enjoy your bus trip."

I still felt as if we were getting punished for missing the plane several days ago. Bad odor or not, eight hours on a jolting bus didn't sound better than zipping up to Addis in one hour. Nevertheless there was no apparent alternative, so Dad and I left immediately for the Jimma bus station, riding in a rattletrap taxi.

When we reached the center market, a young porter threw our cases to the top of a waiting vehicle and we hustled aboard only to discover that virtually every bench was occupied. Not only were the seats taken but every overhead rack and under-seat space was crammed with cloth bundles or bulging bags, even a wicker basket with three trussed chickens.

An old man finally stood up at the back of the bus, moving a cloth satchel into the aisle so that we could squeeze onto his bench. His shoulder bumped into mine as the bus rocked out of the market and began swerving up the escarpment. We were the only Caucasians on the bus—probably the only ones in the last month—which meant we got special scrutiny. A young man who stood in the aisle kept studying my clothes and face, looking away as if fighting his fascination. A two-year-old toddler stared, but when I met his eyes, intrigued by the topknot of hair on his shaved head and the leather amulet strung

148 Fire and Sky

around his neck to fend off spirits, he wailed, burying his brow against his mother's breast. She scowled back at me, probably thinking I had given her son the evil eye.

Unlike these others, the old man who was my seatmate seemed to have no special interest in me. As soon as the bus climbed out of the Jimma valley, he leaned against my shoulder and fell asleep, his woolly head smelling like smoldering wood. My neck ached, but I couldn't shrug the man away for fear he would fall into the aisle. As the bus rocked along the cloud-shrouded slopes, with deep ravines opening below and frothy water rushing over boulders, I tried to stay still enough to let him rest. He didn't actually straighten until two hours later when we reached a checkpoint at a high bridge.

It was here that two sullen sentries came out from behind a bank of sandbags and forced everyone off the bus. And it was here that they forced my father and me to open our suitcases, rummaging around until they discovered his well-marked Bible.

Their disdainful officer stepped up to accost Dad, sneering while he lectured him. "Don't you know this book keeps people sleeping? This stops us from becoming strong."

In response, my father shook his head, smiling broadly. "Why would God want to make us weak?"

Then the soldier curled his lip more rigidly, almost snarling. "What are you? Missionary?"

For Dad to admit that he was what this man despised—a Christian of the Western sort, and evangelistic about it—was to open up to true consequences. Ethiopians had been beaten for less.

Dad nodded, saying, "Yes, I am a doctor, too." And I could see the surly man weighing his options, probably thinking, *You know, it's about time. Why not let one of these capitalist pigs know who is in charge? Why not rough him up like I would any counterrevolutionary? Maybe let the boy get a taste of it?*

I felt the hot Tang at the back of my throat, rancid with dead flesh. Despite all the inspiring stories that I had heard about Ethiopian Christians like Waja and Sahle and Aberash, men and women who refused to hide their faith, I felt an urge to step in front of Dad and apologize, telling the officer that my father couldn't hear well. No, he was not a missionary. The Bible wasn't even ours. We were just bringing it to a friend in Addis, who had left it at our house.

There, by the deep gorge on the road to Addis, I tasted the wretched backwash of my own weakness. I couldn't help a near-panic flood of anxiety. What if we weren't really protected the way I wanted to believe? What if, regardless of his faith, my father would finally be arrested and taken away from me right here at this mountain valley bridge, a hundred miles from anyone who knew us?

"I am letting you go," the officer finally said, "but only because doctor. And I am letting this one go. Is he your son?"

"Yes."

"I am letting him go only because you are doctor." Then he handed the Bible back to Dad as if it smelled bad.

I let out a silent sigh and stepped back. As soon as the bags were closed and on the rack, I followed my father onto the bus, where I could feel everyone staring now—even the old man, who didn't lean onto my shoulder any more. Although I concentrated on the floor or stared out the window, I could sense the lingering heat of their gazes, like the afterburn of an intense day in the sun.

Brave but impractical, that's what my father was. And I felt terribly divided for thinking about him in such terms—ashamed for not being as faithful, but still not sure why he had pulled us all into this hard situation, forcing us to make such difficult decisions. Did my friends back in Troy, Kansas, have to go out the door every morning knowing there was a good chance they would risk their safety for God's honor?

The very next instant, I felt shame again—along with a desire, even a need, to be more courageous. We were here, after all, on a bus in rural Ethiopia surrounded by suspicious strangers, so what good would it do to second-guess? The only real option was to be vigilant and tough. Not to think so much.

I sat rigidly, waiting for what would happen next. Taut and hyper-alert, I listened closely as the bus driver turned on a radio broadcast, and it shifted from instrumental music to a speaking voice. The jazz-like tunes of an electric organ were replaced by a strident man shouting in Amharic. The single loudspeaker was so cracked that it buzzed with each shout, which meant Dad had to listen a long time before being able to interpret. When I whispered, "What is the man saying?" he muttered, "It's a political speech—something about all the workers uniting."

Even without much translation, I could tell that this speech was more than just a routine diatribe. On and on the voice ranted, the tone unmistakably aggressive. And I noticed that the people who had been studying us curiously were now looking away, dropping their gaze when I risked a glance. It was as if they had become afraid to acknowledge we existed.

After the sun set, I stared into the darkness, relieved to no longer be aware of their nervous, look-away eyes. I became so tired at last that I dozed until the bus geared down and I was awakened by pools of light flashing by. Then, at about 10 p.m., the big rocking vehicle finally squealed to a halt in Addis Mercato, headlights illuminating a row of closed stalls.

We climbed down stiffly. Usually a crowd of Addis shoppers would be silhouetted by the light of bare bulbs; vendors would still be carrying trays of cigarettes and candy. But the area seemed utterly abandoned. We had to walk out to the main road to find a taxi, which stopped only after we had been ignored by others.

When at last we reached the mission headquarters and came to the room where Mom and Nat were waiting, she opened the door with a rush and called out, "Hallelujah!" Even though I felt relieved, I was surprised by how even more relieved she seemed. She acted as if some heavy weight had been lifted from her.

"Do the two of you have any idea what day this is?" she asked.

Dad shook his head.

"May Day. The third celebration of the revolution. The army was parading all afternoon, and Mengistu made all residents go to Red Square. The whole city was shut down."

"So that's what we were hearing," Dad murmured.

"You mean they had his speech on the bus?"

When Dad nodded, she blanched. "Do you realize what he did? He actually broke a bottle of blood. He was yelling, 'Down with the imperialists! Down with the American dogs!'"

My holiday, I realized, was officially over.

Scorched

The aggressor, like a mad bull crashing into a ring of flames, will be surrounded by hundreds of millions of our people standing upright. The mere sound of their voices will strike terror into him, and he will be burned to death.

CHAIRMAN MAO

He gave his people over to the sword;
he was very angry with his inheritance.
Fire consumed their young men,
and their maidens had no wedding songs . . . .

PSALM 78.62 – 63

Thirty-Five

Due to the missed flight at Bulki, I was late for the start of the semester and had to be delivered right to Good Shepherd campus. I felt awkward because of the weeks apart from Nancy. After sitting with her at lunch break, wondering what she might be thinking, I finally got a moment alone with her. She surprised me by grabbing my hand and pulling me behind a building. Encouraged, I swung her into my arms for a kiss. Then the two of us leaned against a wall and spilled out the stories of our separate adventures.

At her home on the flatland bordering Sudan, Nancy's father had fitted the family boat with a new motor and taken them fishing. When she described swooping up the muddy waters of the Baro River and having to swerve for surfacing hippos, I shook my head in amazement.

I asked whether they had gotten anywhere near to where the Peace Corps volunteer got munched by a crocodile, and she cocked a coy eyebrow.

"Yeah. In fact, we went swimming."

"You didn't!"

"We did. I mean not right there. But close. It's not a big deal. We know where the crocs hide."

"And what if they aren't in a hiding mood?"

"Then we swim fast!"

Her eyes glittered as she talked. They glittered, too, as I told her about the crazy uphill airstrip at Bulki mountain and how Dad and I arrived in Addis on a bus that featured Colonel Mengistu shouting, "Death to the American Imperialists!"

"Etiopia tikdem!" she added, mocking Mengistu's slogan "Ethiopia first."

There was a sweet intensity to all my reunions that week, unlike anything I had known at Troy High School. Dan Coleman, too, seemed to relish getting back together, laughing with perverse pleasure when I described the dead rat in the water tank. And Dave Iwan chuckled as I told him about the ibis I had shot with my slingshot—how it called out "Char-lee" when it flapped away.

On one of the first afternoons back, Dave and I left our dorm room to wander the fence line, firing slingshots at pigeons high in the eucalyptus trees and exclaiming as rocks went wide, snicking through the leafy canopy.

"So you heard about the doctor who got killed, didn't you?"

I hadn't heard, and it was unsettling to get the specifics, learning that the casualty was one of our own—a missionary named McClure, who was from the same mission as Nancy. I was surprised she had said nothing about this doctor's death, unless she just didn't want to think about it. I didn't want to think about it too much either, still conscious of the vulnerability I felt at the gorge north of Jimma, where the officer accosted my father.

Dave and I reached the far corner of the Bingham Academy campus, right next to a giant swing that had been hanging there ever since we began grade school. Where the ground sloped toward the fence, a long chain hung from a cable between two towering eucalyptus trees, ending with a pole and a crossbar-seat. The school staff had torn down the launching ramp back when we were too small to be allowed onto the swing, so here we were, nearly juniors, and we still had not gotten a proper turn.

"Hey," I proclaimed, "what's stopping us from making our own ramp?" And I pointed to a toppled children's slide.

Dave flashed a gap-toothed grin and ran with me to drag the fallen slide to the crown of the hill, hoisting it onto its wobbly legs. Up I climbed, pulling the seat of the swing into mounting position with a length of twine. At the top, I couldn't quite reach the crossbar-seat, so I had to step onto the handrails of the slide, balancing there and leaning back against the weight of the long chain. I realized that the only way I would ever get onto the swing was to leap out and hoist myself.

For a moment, I looked down at Dave, who was trying to stabilize the swaying ladder, then across the slope into the woods, where

I could see a cluster of tin roofs. Out there, beyond the fence, I realized, was where I had seen the flash of a gun one night, causing me to duck down and bear-walk to safety. With Dave watching, I didn't want to crawl to safety again. This was nothing compared to bullets in the dark, right? So I steeled myself, gathering enough courage to lean forward. And after that there was no recourse but to walk my hands up the pole, swinging my legs into position.

For a second or two I felt completely weightless, a spirit in space. My customary heft did not return until I reached the bottom of the arc and was pushed down onto the crossbar. Then the ground swept by and the G-forces tugged at me, growing heavy as the swing lifted up the other side of the arc.

"Yeaaah," I shouted as I glided up this aerial toboggan run, traveling so high that I swept into a branch and had to kick away.

Riding that swing became a ritual for Dave and me during the first week after Easter holiday. Sometimes we would even take turns before the morning bus could transport us to classes. Doing something so daredevil took the edge off the siege-like atmosphere. And riding the bus on its standard route, lulled back into a familiar schedule, reduced the anxieties that had cropped up on the Jimma-to-Addis trip.

Each morning after breakfast, I joined the twenty other teenagers who piled into the white mid-size bus, and Yared drove us away, letting the boxy vehicle rip down hills in the same confident way, careening past slower vehicles or donkeys. He didn't flinch if forced to squeeze this bulky Fiat past a big truck, despite black gusts of exhaust obscuring oncoming traffic. And he always braked in time for the hard-to-spot kebele checkpoints. Even when steering through a river of pedestrians and herded animals, he would recognize the row of rocks laid out as a marker, or the plain-clothed man stepping out of the crowd with six inches of gun barrel poking up from his shouldered rifle.

With each negotiated checkpoint, I became more at ease. I no longer tensed as Yared slowed for the armed sentries. As soon as he maneuvered back into traffic, accelerating to full speed and gunning around ruts, I joined the others in shouting approval, bouncing high enough to touch the ceiling. On one or two occasions, I even got out my trumpet to play reveille as if leading a cavalry charge.

Twice each day, Yared drove us on these round-trip journeys. And during the first weeks after Easter holiday, he had to make a third trip, coming back to Good Shepherd just before supper time so that he could pick up those of us trying out for the varsity soccer team. I scrimmaged along with the other guys, often playing against Dave Iwan or Dan Coleman. They knew it would be tough for me to make varsity since I had missed six seasons in the United States. Out of solidarity, they even shouted encouragement when I did anything well.

One afternoon I stopped a particularly long goal kick, head-butting it back up the field. "Desta testa," Coleman yelled, which was his coined Amharic term for "happy headie."

"You old sinner," I hissed as he dribbled back toward me and juked his way around. "Repent!"

Despite the political violence all around us, I do not remember being particularly concerned as I raced after Dan that afternoon. I recall instead a cheerful camaraderie. Yes, Dr. McClure had been shot and killed. Yes, Stan Cannata's father was still in prison as a supposed CIA agent, and Iwan's parents were trapped in Jigjiga by a full-scale Somali siege. But no one was talking about such things at school, so I could act, at least for a bit, as if those events were less real or pressing.

I'm sure the staff did not want us to be alarmed. In fact, I imagine they had formed an unspoken pact: keep it positive. The only stories that were passed on to us were inspiring sound bites, the sort of hagiographic accounts that crystallize around a saint. For instance, I recall the tale of an Ethiopian believer in a southern church who was told by an atheist commander that he must call Jesus a dog or electrocute himself by taking hold of a live wire. He chose the wire but, remarkably, all the electricity in the town went dead. Even better, the man who had ordered the possible execution was electrocuted a day later while changing a light bulb.

Maybe I could count on God after all, I thought, each time I heard a story like that, even if it sounded almost too good to be true. Hadn't I already been protected despite my moments of wavering—such as when the officer released Dad and me on the road from Jimma? I

wanted to be stronger, braver. When I wrote in my devotional journal, I declared my loyalty to God—and asked for help to be even
more courageous.

But I wasn't thinking about any of that on the soccer pitch this particular afternoon. I was just immersed in the blissful, distractionless
present, concentrating on the spinning ball and getting myself into
position for the next defensive stand. Dan juked his way around me,
then one of my teammates stole the ball and sent it bulleting down-
field. On the other end, an Ethiopian classmate intercepted it and
sprinted back. He was quicker on his feet than Dan, stepping over
the ball to throw off the first defender, then advancing toward me.
I could headie a ball and I could get in the way. I wasn't much use
otherwise. So I did the one thing that was sure to slow his attack. I
threw myself into a slide tackle.

It wasn't a well-timed slide, unfortunately, so I missed the ball. And
the guy who was dribbling ended up stepping on my ankle at a full
gallop. The effect was excruciating, as if somebody had hammered a
wedge into my joint. I couldn't stand, and the coach decided I must
be taken right away to a clinic across Addis where there was an X-ray
machine.

I cradled that throbbing ankle as a woman staff member drove me
through the streets. I could feel my pulse jolting in the joint, so I had
little patience for stops and starts. When we came upon a crowd of
teenagers who had been released from classes, the jerking became
more pronounced, and by the time our Volkswagen van got to the
center of the crowd, where all the youth seemed to be turned toward
some unseen spectacle, I was gritting my teeth in frustrated pain. I was
not at all prepared to look down and see the body of a boy sprawled
on the asphalt with his books spilled to the side.

This teenager looked as if he had fallen asleep right there—leather
shoes shining in the sun, hair neatly trimmed—except that I could
see a hole in his temple and, under his head, a scarlet pool. Dead.
Nothing theoretical or romantic about it. This was a real boy who was
really dead.

I looked closely and realized he was probably only fifteen or sixteen. Almost exactly my age.

Who had shot him? A classmate who was a gun-toting member

of the local kebele? A rebel assassin who had tagged him as a leader of the school's Marxists? A common criminal who simply wanted a book bag?

Sleep did not come easily that night with my broken ankle in a cast, despite the painkillers I had been given. And in the morning, the road trip to Good Shepherd raised a new vigilance—a kind of hyper-awareness that pulled me out of my usual horseplay. Even if God was overseeing everything at some level, I needed to be more prepared, I decided. More alert, too.

The sour-looking sentries stepped forward like usual, slow and bored, but I watched closely. When they demanded at one check-point that we get off the bus, I could see they were taking their time searching the vehicle, enjoying the power that kept us exposed on the street.

Since I was on crutches, I felt more at risk than ever. "Someone tell me," I suddenly blurted out, "why do we have to stand out here?!"

"Comrade," Iwan muttered, "minim idelem," which was Amharic for "Take it easy; it's no big deal."

"It's not funny, man!"

"No, but this is for the progress of the nation," he replied, his gap-tooth grin turning wicked. "Do not forget: Etiopia tikdem." And he saluted sharply.

I felt ashamed for being so noticeably nervous. I wanted to trust and relax—like I used to. But when we got back onto the bus and started traveling toward Good Shepherd, I didn't feel any of the old ease. In fact, as that week gave way to the next and the next, I remained on a kind of high alert. I found myself watching Yared closely, becoming attuned to the work he was doing. I realized that for all his apparent bravado, he knew how to temper his appearance at each checkpoint. He shifted down, not only changing gears but demeanor. He dropped the wry grin and smart-aleck comebacks. He slid open his side window and leaned out with sober concern. As the kebele sentries slouched toward his window, he greeted them politely, holding his license and travel papers. It became apparent to me that he had been trying, all these months, to not just drive the bulky white Fiat but to act as a buf-fer zone, taking all the heat so we would not have to experience it.

I felt strangely restless with this new perspective, super-conscious all the time. On a Friday one month after I broke my ankle, I tensed up when I realized Yared was taking us home via a slightly longer route that looped along the edge of Addis. Soccer practice had been cancelled, so he had only one afternoon run. I wondered if maybe he was taking this new route because his schedule had been interrupted. In any case, after clearing the guard station above the Addis butcher yard, he accelerated into the valley below, where a flock of kites spiraled over a house-sized heap of cattle bones. The air was rank with spoiled meat, so it was a mercy to pass quickly. Everyone scrunched their noses and shouted, "Go, Yared, go," which encouraged him to keep us barreling along even as we rushed up the next hill, rattling past a little pasture and a stand of eucalyptus trees.

He had just swerved the bus around a pothole when I noticed a sudden movement out of the corner of my eye and realized a man was running from the forest with a rifle. "Yared!" I shouted, and at that same moment, I spotted a sandbag bunker behind this rifleman, where an Ethiopian soldier was training a mounted machine gun on us.

"Yared!" I screamed again, hearing half a dozen voices join in.

The running sentry dropped to a knee and yanked back the bolt of his rifle. Only then did Yared realize the extent of the danger and stomp on the brakes, pushing so hard that the bus shuddered to a stop with dust ballooning out from under it.

The kneeling man rose and raced toward us, still aiming the rifle. Another man erupted from behind the sandbags with an AK-47. Both were yelling in a kind of insulted rage, as if we had thrown manure at them.

For a second, Yared seemed unplugged where he sat, his fists clamped on the wheel. I thought about diving onto the floor. Then Yared came out of his coma and called out, "Everyone off. Now. Now."

With this command I stood up reluctantly and hobbled forward, impeded by the cast on my broken ankle. I regretted being near the front. When the door opened, the rifleman leaped right up the steps, grabbing Yared and jerking him onto the roadside. My roommate was next, and the rifleman swung a foot at him, kicking him the opposite direction. I got the same kick, stumbling on my walking cast.

Yared, off to the side, pleaded with the two sentries in Amharic, but the one with the rifle lunged at him, faking a swing with the butt of his gun. He was a big bull of a man with a blue Kansas City Royals baseball cap and a bulging face. He kept shouting into Yared's ear, pinning him against the side of the bus. Seeing this, the girls from our group balked, which only caused the machine gun guy to shout more loudly, indicating with sideways jerks of the gun that they had to come off the bus too.

"Get in line," whispered Yared as he was pulled back toward us. "Don't move."

So the girls took their places and we all turned stiff as posts, except one girl who couldn't stop shaking and sobbing as the neighborhood cadres flew into a kind of mad lecture, berating us all in Amharic, and saying nothing that I could understand except the occasional curse word like *yetabot*.

My adrenaline was surging. Everything had become sharp-edged and clear. As the machine gun swayed back and forth, my stomach muscles tightened. The girl who couldn't stop crying held out her hands, pleading, "Please please." She choked back a little animal cry, so physically distressed that she began coughing, but I still didn't look down the line. I was aware that the simplest action—just the shifting of weight off the foot in the cast—might be the excuse they needed. It brought to mind the boy on the tarmac with the pool of blood.

The girl stopped coughing and went back to begging, asking them not to hurt us, saying that we were sorry, it was an accident, please let us go.

"They don't even speak English," I wanted to shout. "They can't understand a thing you are saying." However, instead I began to pray to God in an urgent, red-flagged fashion: "Lord, I know you can save us. You saved that guy who took hold of an electric line, so you can do this." And I began to plan what I should do if they opened fire. Drop as if dead? Roll under the bus and run?

My face was tingling. My vision seemed to narrow. Then the sentry with the rifle climbed onto the bus to search, and I realized I hadn't been breathing. I took in a bit of air and, after he brought my trumpet case off the bus and set it down, I took in more air. I stepped forward when Yared asked who the case belonged to. It seemed reassuring to move—to have something practical I could do.

"He wants you to open it," Yared said.

I unclasped the lid and opened the case. The golden instrument lay in bright repose, shining against its plush blue padding.

"He wants to know what it is for," Yared said.

"For making music," I replied, explaining despite the fact that Yared knew exactly what a trumpet was for—having heard me play it on the bus.

The kebele leader lifted the glossy instrument, staring at me as if I smelled worse than the bones and hide rotting down the hill in the butcher yard. His eyes seemed to say, "You pig, what right do you have to own such an expensive toy?"

Then he turned his face to Yared and muttered a few scornful words. He pointed his chin toward us, curling his lip.

Yared made no reply, and the guy with the AK-47 laughed as the rifleman wiped his hands on Yared's chest.

"Ishi," the rifleman said, and I knew at last that we would get out of this with nothing worse happening. "Okay," he was saying, which meant this is over—enough, I'm tired.

He gave Yared a curt command and Yared interpreted: "Everyone onto the bus."

Paradoxically we had a party that evening. Since it was a Friday, we had been given permission to invite a group of friends from Good Shepherd Academy, and they showed up as planned, including Nancy. As we gathered around a small bonfire on the edge of the woods, the checkpoint crisis came up.

"Man, I was already picking out the funeral music," Dan Coleman said.

"Yeah, I thought I was going to have to use my slingshot," Iwan chipped in, and a wave of laughter rippled around the circle.

"You just better be glad some of us were praying," one girl added, which made me think of my own silent prayer, wondering if our pleas might actually be the reason we were alive. On the other hand, what if I had not seen the rifleman running out of the woods? What if the others had not screamed along with me, or Yared had taken a second longer to stomp on the brake? And what about the Ethiopian boy on the tarmac? Had he prayed too?

Nancy cozied up to my shoulder as the fire rose against the darkening night. I liked the feel of her arm against mine and the hypnotic swirl of sparks rising into the black sky. I was almost reluctant, as a result, when my roommate got the idea that he and I should take everybody to the bag swing to demonstrate our takeoff ramp.

"You actually jumped off that thing?" Nancy wanted to know as I hobbled over to watch Dave climb the rickety ladder.

"Why?" I asked, feigning annoyance. "Don't you think I could do it?"

Seeing him fade away in the dark woods then reemerge like a pale ghost made me realize I wanted my own turn. My ankle was no longer aching these days. I had been walking on the cast enough to wear away much of the sole. So I suddenly let go of Nancy's hand and hoisted myself up the ladder, ignoring her cautions.

I lifted the seat of the swing by its string and balanced for a moment on the handrails of the slide, leaning back against the weight of the chain. Then, despite further protests, I let myself tilt forward and fall away. Even though I couldn't leap with the cast, I got onto the crossbar without a hitch, and I was thrilled by the calls from below: "You nuthead. You're gonna kill yourself."

No I was not. Compared to kebele sentries with AK-47s, this was nothing. Here I had some control at least.

I swung into the black forest, letting go of what might have happened if I had not seen the rifleman running out of the woods. Was I alive due to God's protection or my own actions? I couldn't know. Nor could I determine why the dead Ethiopian boy on the asphalt was not as fortunate as me. Or why Dr. McClure was buried now, somewhere in southern Ethiopia.

I could not know, could never know why I was still alive and they were dead. But I felt blissfully safe up there on the swing where God had no reason to take me and where I could rely on the hands and legs I had been given. As I flew back toward the group, I could hear Dan Coleman's voice joining the others. It twanged with sarcastic admiration: "Way to go, weed." And I felt so drunk on my own strange sense of peace that I allowed myself yet another risk. I leaned back and slid my rump off the crossbar so that I was hanging by the back of my knees, ankles crossed at the cast. Then I let go of the pole and hung upside-down.

There was a gasp, and Nancy called out my name. Someone said,

"I can't believe he's doing that," which only made me want to do it more.

I stayed suspended for two or three more swoops, lifting my head and shoulders only at the bottom of the arc so that I would not strike the ground. Although I had nearly died a few hours earlier, I felt so alive and so thankful to be alive, that I was completely happy. I relished knowing that Nancy would shake me in mock anger when I got down, then take my hand in the dark and not let go. I might be an enemy to some. I might not be able to control what would happen tomorrow. I wasn't even sure God would be able to do that. But here, right now, with these few, I felt a closeness unlike anything I had ever known. That solidarity almost made the danger worth it.

Thirty-Six

What a special feeling that was! To swoop back toward the voices of my friends. To return out of darkness into relational refuge. To feel embattled, therefore close as a family.

But memoirs are confessional, so I'll make another confession: I am not a particularly easy person to get close to.

It's a strange thing—this impulse to write a whole book of confessions. It feels intensely personal—so intimate that you might assume memoirists are extremely relational, easy-to-approach people. But I would propose the opposite: often they are isolated people who try to compensate. In fact, their stories may be an eccentric and cautious way of reaching out to form the community they have always desired but rarely been able to enter. They may want to be included as much as anyone else while feeling less adept at actually engaging in shared life.

It's hard to admit how nervous and evasive I can become in person. Give me a pen; I will bare my soul, but put me in a room with a stranger, and I'll hide in a newspaper or ask questions so persistently that the other person never gets a chance to pry anything important out of me. Too intimate, that kind of one-on-one interaction. I instinctively prefer to confess things at a safe remove—like I'm doing here, hoping that you will someday open this book in a place quite far away and get to know me as well or better than my own family.

I suspect that I have always been this way. My relational distance is probably a consequence of being a middle child—always a bit less visible than the proactive first child or the cherished youngest child. It is probably an outworking of extreme introversion, too, which causes me to stand back watching. The watcher doesn't engage much; too busy watching.

Even now I catch myself taking that habitual stance, standing back from my own former self. See that other person I used to be. An odd kid, he was. Look how he used to hide under beds when he was only five or six, trying to create a secret cell of his own, away from the continuous interaction of his family, from the busy ankles clipping by just beyond the fringe of the bedspread. Or see him at twelve years of age, back in Kansas, spotting an after-school friend on the sidewalk. Watch him step behind a garage, prepared to pounce, and then see how he loses the ability to act. See how he stays frozen, a sentinel paralyzed by his own fear of initiating. How he allows his friend to stroll away, humming the tune to "Hey, Hey, We're the Monkees" while swinging a stick at dandelion puffs.

"Do something," I want to shout, as I look back at that other self. "Leap out! Tackle the other kid!" But the moment is gone. Forty years gone, in fact. And the man that I am is the product of that boy. Still a loner, someone who too easily retreats from community, stepping back into the shadows.

Except that there is this weird written attempt to bridge the relational gap—this words-on-paper way of trying not to be so removed. And there is one extreme year in Ethiopia when, as a sixteen-year-old, I felt more united to a group of people than at any other time in my life.

Odd, isn't it, that I would feel such affinity, such tight companionship after only a few months. Quite out of character, don't you think? So why the sudden anomaly?

Some of it might have been that in Ethiopia, I was back with a community where I actually belonged—back with the clan that would claim me. In fact, I felt that sensation as soon as we arrived at Bingham Academy. Ah, my people. Not just the ones who had been my friends in second and third grade, like Mari Dye or Dan Coleman, but the whole extended family of displaced children with hyper-religious parents—surrogate siblings brought together by a shared away-from-home existence.

"Missionary Kids" we were called, and years later (even decades later) we would still be claiming that moniker as if we had never quite grown out of being children. "So you are an MK, too!" I might say while talking with some thirty-something adult who grew up in India or Peru, using those two initials for a code-like sense of bonding, two mysterious letters that would indicate how we had a whole way of life that was ours alone.

Take that affinity, though, and double it—because in 1977 the MKs in Ethiopia were twice as set apart, viewed as enemies of the state and treated with suspicious hostility by those who believed the new political rhetoric. Since we were unusually cut off, we often had only each other to trust, which gave us a paradoxically intense and meaningful connection—a bond so strong that for me, as an introverted youth, it was almost intoxicating.

I have never, since that year in Ethiopia, felt as connected to a group relationally. In fact, I suspect that the experience only made me more aloof in unintended ways. After all, if our besieged closeness became the standard for community, how could I find community here in America as a majority member—just another White Anglo-Saxon Protestant in the suburbs of Des Moines? What could measure up to my ideal?

The disappointment and frustration eventually made me defeatist. How does one connect with other parents on the sidelines of a soccer field, even if all the kids happen to go to the same school or live in the same neighborhood (which they don't)? Or how does a person bond with neighbors who are always coming and going in their cars and only once or twice a year gathering for a block party, eating hot dogs and drinking beer in the no-man's land of the street?

Even in church I tend to feel this resignation. How do I, with all the awkward attempts to go deeper in conversation, feel true solidarity there? What matters enough to warrant a follow-up conversation?

I remember now how attracted I sometimes felt toward minority students back when I first became a college teacher at Kansas State University. My wife and I had moved to a town in the middle of Kansas, and I felt stabs of loneliness as I passed by a cluster of Chinese students talking in Mandarin, so attentive to each other, so much more unified than the swirling crowd of whites around them.

The same sensation would be triggered sometimes when I noticed a group of African American students congregated on one side of the campus cafeteria, separate from the larger chaos. Suddenly I would be swept by an irrational desire to join them, wanting to feel "different," no longer lost in the majority. There was laughter in their midst, and catcalls and bumping fists and acknowledgement of a shared uniqueness that felt so familiar I wanted to join right in, to be in solidarity the way I had once felt, too. However, I was doomed to stand outside. I could only watch, not unlike those children who had congregated outside the fence of my boarding school in Addis Ababa. If I had tried to catch someone's attention, halting the fist-bumping and the jokes, I would have sounded just as out of place, I'm sure: "Hey you, my friend. Whad-dis your name?"

So I turned away and walked on, blending into the crowd, mourning a loss that they might never guess, a loss that even I could not understand. It is a loss that only now seems obvious as I look back over the decades and recognize the way I have always, since Ethiopia, felt a strange separation from others—a kind of automatic sense of being a foreigner even when I look like I belong.

Thirty-Seven

Danger was something I could expect now. After the near-disastrous checkpoint, it was all too clear.

What I did not anticipate were the sudden grief-inducing erasures. The first came without warning, announced by my parents. One day they were living on the mountain near Bulki; the next they were standing in my dorm room telling me I would probably never see that home again. They had been evacuated.

"The mission gave us twenty-four hours," Mom said, as if apologizing.

"But why?"

She sighed and looked at Dad. Then she tried to go further, "They just don't think it's safe anymore, not for a family."

"I thought it was supposed to be off the radar?"

I stopped speaking when I saw the anguish on my mother's face. Then my father tried to pull himself out of his own funk, turning to face me instead of gazing out the window. He described what led up to the evacuation. Apparently, the whole Gamo Gofa province had proven more volatile than anticipated. At another station thirty miles from Bulki, the turnaround had come quickly, prompted by a bullying gebere commander, who told the missionaries to leave or stay forever—in graves. However, as soon as the missionaries started packing, the paid staff flew into reaction, worried about losing their jobs. The whole community became convinced something criminal was occurring, and a suspicious crowd wouldn't let any of the alarmed foreigners out of their houses, not even after a plane arrived to take them away.

Mr. Cumbers, the director of our mission, did not want a similar situation at Bulki—with the suddenly unemployed staff holding hostages, not releasing them until the mission paid two years' worth of severance salaries. After negotiating the release of those other house-arrested missionaries, he reasoned it would be best to extract my parents without announcing their departure. Then his plan became necessity; Missionary Aviation Fellowship sent a memo announcing that they were going to pull out of Ethiopia. Since the government was demanding seats on MAF flights and dictating where the planes could fly, the pilots feared they would lose the whole fleet if they didn't act immediately.

"We didn't have any idea this was coming," Mom said. "They just radioed, saying there would be one last flight and we had to be on it."

In fact, the radio operator insisted it could not look like an evacuation. "Pack only two suitcases," she explained. "Burn any records that might incriminate locals. And be ready at the airstrip by 6:30 a.m. when the plane will draw less attention."

As my parents described their last twenty-four hours at Bulki, I could picture the immense open space beyond the station, and I could see the kites soaring. I could practically feel the wind ruffling my shirt-sleeves. With sad nostalgia, I recalled the gentle way the church elder set down his teacup while asking for Amharic New Testaments, and how the minister at the savannah church laughed as I leaned back and wiped my brow, overcome by spicy doro wat.

My face must have betrayed my disappointment because my parents insisted that they really had no choice. This was not the way they wanted to go. They explained that though they feared retaliation, they couldn't disappear without telling someone why they were leaving. They chose Joseph, the dresser, and as they handed him envelopes with several months' worth of salary for him and the part-time gardener, he just nodded calmly, even sympathetically. In fact, he offered to go down the mountain that night so that he could deliver their mimeograph machine to the church in the valley. That way, he explained, it could be used to make Christian materials instead of being confiscated by the Marxists.

So Joseph returned to the house after sunset and put the machine on his shoulder, all forty pounds of angular metal, covering it with a dirty rag before striding away into the dusk. Then my parents went to work destroying records that could be used as evidence against any local Christians or patients who might be targeted for associating with the mission. For an hour or more, they tossed patients' charts and bookstore orders into the blazing fireplace, fearing that someone might notice telltale sparks flying from the chimney. They were conscious that the head of the local farmers' association had come to their door only a few days earlier seeming uncharacteristically agitated.

"I am sorry but I must look into your house," he had told them. "I have been ordered." Then he had strolled from room to room with his antique carbine over his shoulder, not sure what he was after until he noticed binoculars on the windowsill and picked them up.

"I must take these," he said. "It is the rules."

Dad had tried to explain that he used the binoculars only for watching birds, but the man simply repeated as if reciting memorized lines, "I must take these, so that no one can use them for bad reason."

Now, as they shoved medical files and church correspondence into the blaze, they felt grief at erasing the connection between them and the people of the area. While the names on the sheets of paper crumbled to ash and fluttered up the chimney, Mother wept, feeling guilty about walking away from fellow Christians who had no way to escape. It seemed they were betraying the entire legacy of the church at Bulki, not just their own work but the dozens of years of dedicated work by other missionaries and evangelists and local ministers—doctors and nurses, too—who had built the clinic and treated thousands of patients.

Mom said that she looked around the little bungalow in complete anguish, noting china plates that had probably been brought up the mountain twenty or thirty years earlier in sawdust-stuffed crates, strapped to mules. She saw the living room bookshelf with decades of accumulated favorites, and the battery-powered phonograph with its outdated records. She felt she might as well put a match to the whole house; she was practically building a funeral pyre to half a century of combined effort.

"Maybe we should pick one or two things that represent it all," Dad suggested. "You know, something we can fit in the suitcases." So the two of them made individual selections: a delicate teacup with a floral design, plus a book of Christian poetry inscribed to the father of the family who had occupied the house before us.

There was a strange comfort in packing these symbolic items, Mom explained, because each one represented colleagues who were forced to leave the Bulki compound earlier. In the case of the teacup, she wondered if it had belonged to her old mentor at missionary candidate school, Mrs. Forsberg, who might have received it as a wedding gift. The amazing thing about that possibility was that while the Forsbergs had been forced to evacuate Bulki during World War II, here were my parents doing the same thing now, thirty-five years later. Maybe there would be another generation to return, they thought. And maybe the Christians at Bulki would prove themselves as strong as the Wolaittan Christians during World War II, who grew from a handful to ten thousand while the missionaries were away. Maybe, in fact, it wasn't even about missionaries anymore, they reasoned, which heartened them both before they finally went to bed at three in the morning, trying to get just two hours of sleep.

Of course, a teacup and a book of Christian verse were not going to raise much suspicion if my parents had to open their bags on departure. What worried them as they began their morning hike to the airstrip was the bulky mission radio that they had been instructed to bring back. Joseph had already returned from carrying the mimeograph machine into the valley, and he hoisted the boxed equipment onto his shoulder in the pale dawn light. His kindness was inexplicable, almost painful to witness. It made them both want even more to get this departure over with. And when the plane set down as scheduled, with only one or two farmers hiking past, Mom and Dad were relieved to think that the awful tension was almost over. Unfortunately, though, the pilot grimaced and explained that they would have to wait because the engine battery needed to cool.

For an agonizing forty minutes my parents sat on the grassy airstrip with Joseph, waiting while a shepherd boy fetched a bucket of water and the pilot dunked the overheated battery. A small crowd formed, attracted to the aircraft's long aluminum wings and bladed propeller. Then the head of the farmers' association came jogging with his rifle, and he asked nervously to look in their bags.

"What do you think your dad showed him first?" Mom asked as she was recounting this part of the saga.

"The radio?"

"Exactly. Of all things, he went right to that cardboard box and opened it!"

Dad shrugged as she went on. "Thank God for guardian angels. I think your father has three—because that man seemed to not even see inside the box."

The head of the farmers' association flipped through the suitcases haphazardly, letting Mom and Dad buckle them shut. Then he let my parents climb into the plane. The engine was already roaring when the pilot shouted to them, "By the way, one of the boxes we unloaded is not medical. It's got about a hundred Amharic New Testaments. I think you ordered those for a local church?"

"Charles!" Mom shouted as he undid his seatbelt and opened the door of the plane. "Just leave it. They'll get it sorted out." She knew that sometimes simply owning a translation of a Bible not sanctioned by the Orthodox church could get a person arrested.

Nevertheless, Dad hopped out of the plane and shouted into Joseph's ear that this one box should go to the mountain church we had visited as a family—to be taken care of by the white-haired elder who came to our house.

Of course, the leader of the gebere stepped forward to see what had caused the hullabaloo, but Dad reached right into the box, handing him one of the Amharic New Testaments. He told the man, "I think you will enjoy it. This book holds all the wisdom for life."

My mother watched from the roaring plane, half-paralyzed. The tense lieutenant turned the little book over in his hand, surrounded by curious farmers. It was close to the size of another little red book that had started to be distributed all over the countryside, full of Chairman Mao's sayings. My mother prayed that the man might confuse it with that book. He flipped it open, fluttering the pages. Then he smiled, glad for Dad's generosity. "Amasuganalow!" he shouted, offering his thanks over the snarl of the whirling propeller. He even helped to lift the box of New Testaments onto Joseph's shoulder.

"Is there some chance," he asked as Dad stepped back toward the plane, "that you could help pay a little for our farmers' association?"

"Tenish?" the man added, using the Amharic word for just a little bit.

He had hold of my father's hand with both hands, so Dad had no option but to make some sort of response. "I cannot make any promises," he shouted, "but I will ask our director in Addis. Ishi?"

And so that is how my parents left—having given the local Marxist a Bible and having promised to look into whether the mission could help to fund his cadre.

When the tale was over, my parents stood there in my dorm room, as if not in the right scene. They scanned the space awkwardly, searching for something they recognized. Now I understood why they had left Bulki, but I still felt stunned. As I stared out the window toward the tin-covered fence of the school, grief rose in my throat, and I had to work to force it down. Even if I had spent only a few weeks at the Bulki station, sometimes overwhelmed by its remoteness, I still mourned for what might have been. I had begun to look forward to flying back with my brother Nat and picking up where we left off—exploring down the mountain, visiting the church in the valley, eating injera ba wat with the elders.

"What about buses?" I demanded, despite the haunting memory of the scornful officer at the gorge above Jimma. "Couldn't we just go back that way?"

They shook their heads. Even if there was a bus route near to Bulki, the mission wouldn't let us.

"So where are they going to put us? Back here in Addis?"

They nodded. As it turned out, my parents had already been asked to oversee a compound in Addis, where the mission was developing a hostel for famine-relief workers. Since the northern drought was still forcing villagers into famine camps, the mission had created a special relief unit composed of young Westerners and Ethiopian nationals who traveled in and out of the camps. The headquarters for those workers, when they came into the capital to rest up, was this Community Development House, or CD House, and my mother and father would be the official house parents.

I frowned. For relief workers this urban compound might be a reprieve, but for me it meant staying trapped in Addis. Great, I thought, more of the same—gunshots all night and checkpoints all day.

I really didn't think things could get worse—except that a few days later the principal at Good Shepherd announced that the Academy would be closing permanently at the end of the year. Supposedly too few students would remain. Also, the government wanted the land.

How could this be happening, I wondered. Where would we all study next year? In temporary classrooms at Bingham?

I had no idea just how much this final change was going to affect the future—not until the first contingent of missionaries announced that they were joining the exodus out of Ethiopia. The Colemans decided to take a year's furlough in Canada. The Iwans were leaving too. The Cannatas. The McElroys. The Dyes. Then Nancy came to me one afternoon almost trembling with her news: "We're leaving too."

Thirty-Eight

Community is something we all want. Yes, we may feel a stronger desire at times to individuate, stepping away to form a distinct self; psychologists agree that we are driven to have agency, not just intimacy. However, psychologists also insist that we cannot live without other humans. We long for connection and need it even if we find it frustrating.

So here's the paradoxical blessing of belonging to a small, shunned minority: a remarkable sense of kinship.

Strangely enough, to be excluded by the majority in Ethiopia meant to feel wonderfully included by the rest—both the fellow missionary youth at boarding school and the Ethiopian church community. To be judged and ostracized by some meant to feel accepted and appreciated by others. And so when I saw all that hard-earned solidarity beginning to shatter, I was undone.

Decades had to roll by before I would admit that one of the other paradoxical beauties of being in such a small and separate community was its exclusivity. Perhaps I wouldn't let myself acknowledge our exclusivity because it seemed such a standard part of "belonging." Look at how most groups use separation as a way to define themselves: sororities not fraternities, skateboarders not jocks, country western listeners not alternative rockers, Baptists not Catholics, Democrats not Republicans. Look how early it starts too—with childhood "clubs" that have a secret hideout or password. Only a few allowed in. Everyone else out.

However, it seems apparent to me now that the missionary experience can magnify that exclusivity greatly. To begin with, a missionary leaves an original home clan, setting aside normal relational bonds. Then a missionary willfully becomes "different," defined against a culture that, at first, is likely to scrutinize or reject. Next, a missionary tries to form a separate community on abstract terms—at first with a small group of fellow missionaries who are yoked ideologically, then with local converts who adopt the new beliefs and become bonded through the same transcendent allegiance to something they hold higher than their own language or customs or food or clothing. Together, they are united by an essential shared meaning, a meaning that is supposedly for everyone while at the same time operating as a separating identifier—the source of "us" rather than "them." Password? "No one comes to the Father except by me."

My middle-aged, more aware self hates to admit it, but as a sixteen-year-old Christian Westerner in Ethiopia, I actually loved being inside that circle of shared allegiance! I still miss it at some primal self-centered level, which leaves me feeling disconcerted.

The last time I went to a reunion of former MKs, organized by a few classmates who decided to host us in Dallas, I was reminded over and over of the exclusivity that had once been a source of our close-knit comfort. This time, though, the same ideology felt like confinement—at least for me as the person I had become. George W. Bush was running against John Kerry for a second term in the White House, and almost all of my old classmates—with a few exceptions like my Canadian friend Daniel Coleman or my Mennonite friend Karen—were marching in lockstep in support of Bush despite the fact that he had started a war against Iraq based on flimsy evidence of supposed weapons of mass destruction.

Although Bush had brought death to tens of thousands in an unnecessary war that had no real link to the attack on the World Trade Center towers, those former missionary kids upheld him as the only viable presidential candidate because he was firm, because he wasn't afraid to say who was good or evil, and because he was preserving babies from abortion. Never mind that thousands of people were dying unnecessarily on the other side of the globe; they were convinced that Islam must be stopped at all costs. As for Kerry, who had served in the Vietnam War and taken a strong stand protesting against it, he was a waffler. My former classmates were all the more convinced because he claimed to be a practicing Catholic. Who could trust a Catholic, after all? Who could really trust one ever since Martin Luther?

The reunited remnant of our class wanted to have a shared wor-

ship service on the last day of the reunion, a Sunday, and they invited
two clergy, both men who had married into the clan, to lead the service. One of those elected preachers, in the grip of his own passionate
prayer, blurted out, "You alone, Lord, are righteous. And Lord, we
just pray that you will bring to light the deeds of the wicked. Drag
them into the open, Lord, and if they will not repent, smite them with
the sword."

Who were these wicked, I wondered. And just how literal the
sword?

Was he praying for victory over the Iraqis? Or over pretenders like
John Kerry, in the thrall of the old Anti-Christ-in-disguise, the pope?
Even more alarming, was he praying for the destruction of liberal,
abortion-accepting mainstream Protestants like the Episcopalians I
worshipped with? Was I myself deserving of this sword, now that I
not only attended an Episcopal church but was married to—horror
of horrors—a female priest?

This was a double loss for me: to feel the old idealized bond broken
between me and that ring of friends, and to stand outside the closing
circle, watching my space snap shut. As teenagers, we had been pulled
apart by a revolution. Due to the vagaries of our multinational back-
grounds, we had been plucked away to places as distant as Canada
and Norway, New Zealand and Central African Republic. But I had
thought—or at least hoped—that we would stay united in point of
view, closely linked by our shared experience and mutual understanding. Fellow MKs forever.

Even though I had changed over the years, I guess I had assumed
they were changing similarly. Hadn't they also seen the damages of
war, realizing how much it should be avoided unless absolutely necessary? And hadn't they seen people who lived by different values, learning to respect those differences enough not to rush into judgment
or conflict? Hadn't they, for that matter, formed a similar underdog
appreciation for people from poorer, less-developed nations, understanding why they might resent U.S. interference? Given our shared
background, how could we have come to such different conclusions?
How could we have drifted so far apart?

Thirty-Nine

At the end of my sophomore year, in response to the losses that were beginning to be felt—the friends packing up and flying away—I did the only thing I could do: I created my own convenient illusion. Since I wanted to keep my community, I convinced myself it would happen. My imagination wove the scenarios into being. New families would come to Ethiopia just like we had done. The administrators at Good Shepherd would see that there were enough students to keep the school open. Dan's parents and Nancy's parents would reverse their decisions. Who knew? Maybe a coup would bring a new government—some shiny democratic republic with a parliament of representatives from all the tribes of Ethiopia.

At graduation the seniors danced with their diplomas, then cried. I decided to be a cheerful bystander. This was normal. High school was over for them. Aside from losing my roommate's older brother, I would not be terribly affected. So I went on buttressing my unspoken hopes, resolved to get what I wanted: the chance to come back after the holidays and continue. After Nancy left for Gambela, where her parents were preparing to relocate to the States, I just clung to the fact that we would see each other in six weeks when they came back through Addis. Surely something would change by then—some answer to my prayers.

Nat and I vacated our dorm rooms, moving across Addis to the Community Development House, where Mom and Dad had been reassigned. I treated this shift like a normal hiatus. At least our new home was on the grounds of an unusually beautiful estate, made available because the owner, a coffee magnate, had decided that he should distance himself from his vacation villa during the communist shakedown.

The main building was a palatial cut-stone mansion with columns. A long drive looped from the gate to the front steps, bending round a sward of green grass where clusters of palm trees hung down, heavy with dates. There was also a hedged garden with a grid of gravel walks, and though the roses were overrun, it had a certain charm because of its growing wildness! Plus, the pines that boxed it in were stocked with doves, which gave Nat and me something to shoot with our slingshots.

I missed the unlimited openness of Bulki, but I knew this place was as good as it would get in crowded Addis. We had large enough grounds to kick a soccer ball, and we had the privacy of our own separate house, a low-slung building that had served as a former servant quarters.

Nat and I set up our bedroom in a glassed-in sunporch at the end of the small house, where Mom had hung curtains for privacy. As we shifted the bunk bed and dresser to make room for a throw rug, we saw several young Ethiopian men passing by, arriving through the front gate with duffle bags. Mom explained that they were famine-relief workers checking in at the main building, which had been turned into a suite of guest rooms with a meeting hall and a dining area. We would eat most of our meals over there, she added, since she was in charge of the kitchen.

I wasn't excited about spending mealtimes with a group of strangers, so that first week I kept to myself after polite greetings. I was more enthused when I went to church at Headquarters because I knew I might get to see a few remaining friends. However, the only one to show up kept focusing on the one thing I didn't want to acknowledge: the exodus of missionaries. He talked especially about his own imminent departure and his family resettling in Kenya, not far from Nairobi. As he got into the car beside his brother, he called back, "So I'll see you at Rift Valley Academy in a couple months, right?"

I lifted my thumb, trying to act positive, but I was shaking my head internally, thinking, *This can't be happening. Somehow, it's going to turn around.*

The next Sunday, it was Dan Coleman's turn to say good-bye, too, and I had an even harder time fending off reality because he wasn't holding up the hope of seeing me again.

"Don't be such a weed," I argued. "Your parents can't stay away.

You know it. Good Shepherd will reopen — or Bingham will add high school classes. If nothing else, we'll go to Rift Valley and be room-mates."

He just grimaced.

Distressed, I wrote letters to Nancy, penning them on the tissue-thin blue aerograms that might or might not get delivered by the government DC-3s. When a letter finally arrived back, I was dismayed to read this note on the outside: "The plane just came and I was hoping to hear from you, but there was no mail. Write soon!"

Inside, she explained that her parents were trying to decide what to pack and what to sell or get rid of, including their well-used electric ice-cream machine. "We made some ice cream, and I thought of you while I ate it. It's so nice and green down here and the river's coming up. I wish you could be here to see."

Saddened by our separation, I moped around the bedroom for a day or two, listening to music cassettes on the speakers I had built at the Headquarters woodshop. I stared at the ceiling cracks and crooned along with Karen Carpenter's strangely nostalgic love song "We've Only Just Begun." Then I got sick of my sorrow and went out with Nat to kick a soccer ball.

At the main building across the gardens, more workers had been coming and going, driving off to areas affected by the prolonged drought. Part of me wished I could go along. They were mostly Ethiopian men, but also Canadian, American, and Australian. And there were even a few women, including a freckly, robust Irish woman who was clearly falling in love with one of the Ethiopian workers and could be seen lounging on the grass with him when the two were on leave. As Nat and I kicked the soccer ball, we heard her laughing heartily or noticed her going quiet, her eyes locked on his. Their affection intensified my own lovesickness, but at the same time I was impressed with how the two of them were crossing over the unspoken racial barrier that older missionaries kept.

This new generation of missionaries, labeled "development workers," was actually a kind of sleight of hand that Sudan Interior Mission was trying to play on the increasingly rigid government. Since visas were being given only to people with technical or professional skills, the mission had started to bring in agriculturalists and engineers and such. The idea was to keep a kind of disguised presence in the country as the traditional church-planting missionaries were denied visas.

What no one had anticipated, however, was the way this new breed of workers might alter the mission endeavor. With their well-drilling rigs and food programs, they were much more concerned with social justice and much less concerned with protocol. The same was true for their Ethiopian peers—a young generation of staff workers who had already survived four years of Mengistu's revolution. Tough and resilient, these young nationals were daring to speak their mind in ways that the older generation never would.

I learned about their candid style in my own teenage manner—during mealtimes at the guesthouse, when conversations were full of rowdy verbal sparring. Since Nat and I ate with them, we had ringside seats. The food was almost always injera ba wat, which suited me fine, and I listened closely as I savored the sourdough crepes and peppery stews, trying to figure out the Amharic comebacks that got the best laughs. I stayed quiet except to ask for an occasional translation. Then the Ethiopian guys looked at me as if I was a pesky little brother. They liked to taunt me—their junior by five or ten years—with the spiciest of dishes, chuckling as I tried to work my way through a solid chili pepper, wiping my eyes.

I took such teasing with a grin. I wanted to prove myself. But I was completely unprepared one afternoon for an outburst that came from one of the quieter guys, a fierce fellow who happened to be sitting across from me eating from the same platter.

"Why do you do that?" Tekola demanded as I tore off some injera and prepared to pinch a potato out of the *alicha* stew.

I looked back in genuine confusion. "Do what?" I asked.

"Use both hands?"

"I don't know."

"But you should know. What is wrong with you? The right hand is for food. The other is dirty!"

The whole table went quiet, captive to a kind of charged embarrassment. I noticed right away that no one was reprimanding Tekola, so I surmised that I must have been offending others as well. My father had to explain later that the left hand was seen as the hand for the toilet, and that in Ethiopia, since everyone ate from the same platter, left hands should stay in the lap.

In some odd way that honest challenge broke through a kind of invisible bubble that had insulated me during the months in boarding school, where I could see the Ethiopian culture nearby without really joining it. Yes, kebele sentries might confront me, but Tekola's critique was a different sort of confrontation that deserved a different response. I found myself simply wanting to be more clued in. I ate carefully with only my right hand, and I became more alert to Amharic words and customs. I grew curious a week later when a visiting speaker came to the CD House to lead a kind of underground conference. Drawn to his voice booming out of the meeting hall, I slipped into the crowded space. I stood at the back behind all the folding chairs and listened as he built his argument in chanted Amharic.

A translator was trying to keep up with the rush of words: "In theory, Jesus would approve of many Marxist ideas. Blessed are the poor, he said. Go and give all you have to those who are in need. It is harder for a rich man to enter the kingdom of God than for a camel to pass through the eye of a needle."

The listeners nodded soberly, murmuring "Amen."

"But Jesus would never let a sparrow fall without being numbered. This is the same Lord who said even the hairs on your head are numbered. He is the one who cares for every individual, not just the masses."

"Getah yemeskin," the listeners shouted, meaning, "The Lord be praised."

My mother came out from the kitchen, and I leaned over to ask the speaker's name.

"Solomon Abate," she whispered. "You've probably heard him on the radio. He was the announcer at Radio Voice of the Gospel until the government took it."

Aha, I thought, and I listened more closely as Mom explained that Solomon was one of the main reasons the government had seized the station. In fact, it was probably him that the higher-ups were responding to in the blunt report published by the official newspaper of the Derg. There they had given their rationale for nationalizing the radio station: "The radio is one of the means utilized by imperialism for subverting popular revolutions. Through radio stations imperialist forces not only belittle but also ridicule the march of progressive societies."

I needed no newspaper now to tell me that Solomon truly was challenging the march of this "progressive society." And I was fascinated as a result. From what Solomon said, it was apparent that he was on a blacklist. According to him, he had been speaking at another recent gathering when an unfamiliar man walked up, aimed a pistol, and fired.

"The bullet was stopped by God," the translator said, trying to keep up with Solomon's galloping narrative. "It left the gun, but never arrived. In fact, the assassin was so surprised he just stood there. Then he jumped through a window and ran. He fled because he knew he could not win against God."

"Egzhiaber yemeskin!" murmured the listeners.

"There is no God like our God," the translator added as Solomon rushed on. "The communists say they have no religion, but they do. They believe in the god of Marx. They follow the religion of revolution. But their god is dead, and their faith can only lead to destruction."

"Awo," rumbled the crowd, in a mass "yes."

No one talked so openly, challenging the very basis of the new government, and I found myself looking around the room with alarm, wondering which one of these listeners might leap forward with a pistol now—perhaps an unfamiliar face in the third row or, worse, someone who had been eating meals by my side?

In only a few more weeks, Solomon would flee across the border into Kenya disguised as a peasant, but I could already sense why this had to happen. He was the sort of threat the government most feared: a true counterrevolutionary, the sort of rebel who would revolt against the revolution, unafraid to combat one ideology with another.

Seeing the curtains billow behind him, I wished that someone would close the windows, sealing in his voice. At the same time, I was thrilled at his audacity—and at the defiance that we shared by simply leaving the windows open. For the moment, I felt invigorated, thinking that we had something here that was more powerful than all the violent force of the Derg. Maybe, just maybe, we could fight back.

Forty

O ne hard but good benefit of being deprived of my boarding school community was that, perhaps for the first time, I could not ignore the Ethiopian community around me. Missionary children, for numerous reasons, can get cut off from the culture of their host country. The main problem, of course, is that mission schools serve as a kind of disengaged refuge where everyone eats Western food and studies Western history and listens to Western music, creating a little colony of detached imported life.

Bingham Academy and Good Shepherd had certainly provided that island existence for me—an oasis of cultural security in the otherwise harsh surroundings. In one way I am quite thankful. Our parents, for good reason, wanted to protect us from the storm—to give us a good education in a safe environment. Nevertheless, because of the cultural remove of those boarding schools, I had not really engaged with many Ethiopians during the half year in Addis. At Bulki, perhaps, but otherwise I was sequestered, surrounded by an embattled circle of fellow missionary youth who, by necessity, banded together.

Stripped of that close community, I was at a loss and very unhappy, yet I was finally in a position to form relationships with Ethiopians who could be peers—young people who didn't show me the deference of elder Ethiopians. I sensed a remarkable unity within that group of relief workers, and not a closed unity. Their shared beliefs really did trump cultural differences, linking them closely to my parents, who would still be receiving calls and emails from Tekola and Solomon and Sehin decades later, despite the separation forced on us by the war. Their values made them look on other individuals as equals, regardless of class or race, and that understanding gave them personal dignity while motivating them to assist those who were at the risk of losing dignity, such as the famine victims whom others considered a lost cause.

The Ethiopian Marxists were another story. I wasn't experiencing much openness or respect from them, nor did I see much respect toward fellow Ethiopians. Even though the needs of famine victims had been used as a tool to bring down the emperor, which implied an underlying concern for the welfare of all Ethiopian people, the actual individual on the street was more at risk after the revolution than before.

That's the basic incongruity with your typical Marxist revolution, at least in my opinion: it is so concerned with the needs of the masses that it will violate the rights of individuals, even whole groups of individuals. Yes, theoretically, what is good for the masses is good for everyone, but in the process of reaching that abstract "good," the individual's needs may be shoved aside. In fact, many, many individuals may end up sacrificed on the altar of the masses.

Just consider how each of the classic Marxist revolutions began. In each case, there was a period of public scapegoating, during which those who had ruled or amassed wealth, no matter how decent they might have been, were treated as enemies, bringing shame and guilt down onto everyone, including those who were forced to merely stand and watch. Early in the Russian revolution, the whole society had to witness suspected enemies of the new republic executed en masse as retaliation for an assassination attempt on Lenin. In Petrograd alone, five hundred supposed "class enemies" (most of them intelligentsia and capitalists, and therefore part of the despised bourgeoisie) were rounded up and shot even though the would-be assassin came from a member of a parallel socialist party.

Within another three or four years, another fifty thousand intellectuals and former landowners were carted off to concentration camps as suspected dissidents, in effect getting turned into government-owned slaves of the Soviet Republic, a source of unpaid labor for digging Arctic canals or clearing forests. And by the end of Stalin's rule thirty years later, that number had ballooned dreadfully. Records suggest that over fourteen million people passed through the ever-expanding labor camps, among them the author Aleksandr Solzhenitsyn, who

did eight years of forced work in mines and on construction crews—
all because he had made a few veiled criticisms of Stalin in personal
letters while serving as a Red Army captain during World War II.

Fear was the ethos of the typical Marxist revolution, which demanded complete public loyalty. The same was true of the Maoist
revolution in China. Landlords and wealthier members of society
were marched into the streets with placards that shamed them. They
were beaten in public.

And in Ethiopia? It was no different. In the service of a higher
public good, unsuspecting citizens were forced to relinquish their
property, to settle in newly formed cooperatives, to labor in huge
development schemes. All Ethiopians, regardless of personal inclina-
tions, were made to carry their proper government passes, to turn out
for staged celebrations, to hold up the placards and shout slogans—
because who knew who might be watching?

So it was quite remarkable that by 1977, three years into the Ethiopian revolution, someone like Solomon Abate would dare to voice
criticism or resistance, even if doing it secretly. It was remarkable, too,
that other people would show up and sit in the same room, calling
out their affirmation. Out on the streets, by contrast, everyone had
learned to pull in close and whisper. In fact, by the time we flew out
of Ethiopia, landing at the national airport in Kenya, I would panic
simply from hearing people speaking loudly, apparently unconcerned
who might be listening. *Let's get out of here*, is what I thought. *Let's leave
this building before the authorities swoop in.*

Forty-One

The "small rains" had passed, and now the big rains settled in, drenching Addis with heavy downpours, so that the ravine behind the house filled with rusty torrents. Between cascades Nat and I shot slingshots, getting doused if pigeons broke from cover and shook down the pendant water. Then after a while we were forced back inside by another downpour, or we ran to the main building with an umbrella so we could eat another meal where the development workers were coming and going, talking about the famine in the drier, drought-ridden north.

One evening, Mom and Dad came to our bedroom and said they had some important news: they had decided Nat and I would definitely attend Rift Valley Academy in the coming year. They said there was a good chance, too, that we would all be reassigned to another country, probably Sudan.

This announcement sent me into a deep depression. I had subconsciously begun to expect the shift to another boarding school, but I had not allowed for the very real possibility that my parents would leave Ethiopia, forcing us to start over. I pictured Sudan as an endless series of sand dunes with blowing dust and not a tree in sight. The only person I knew who had lived there, a senior from Good Shepherd Academy, had joked that it was the armpit of Africa, which seemed rude, but didn't make me at all interested in visiting the country.

That night, after we had eaten at the main building, I became more irritated as Mom and Dad announced they had invited guests to our house. Guests would mean appearing cheerfully interested. I sulked in my room and stayed there even after the front door opened and I heard murmured conversation. Mom finally came looking for me, and I protested: "Why do I have to meet them? They're your friends, not mine."

She just stared, arms crossed and one eyebrow lifted, so at last I got up from the bed and followed her into the main room, where Dad was stoking a wood fire against the dampness. To my surprise, the man next to him was an Ethiopian in a tan uniform, obviously a military officer. This changed things. I wasn't sure what to make of a military man in our house.

He got up and shook my hand politely, giving his name as Yeshiwas, the Amharic version of Jesus. He articulated each word with precise English that didn't quite match the accent of other English-speaking Ethiopians. His light-brown face was lined with premature wrinkles and his short hair salted. He seemed almost embarrassed to be here, as if he had come to the wrong door.

Then a knock sounded and the man relaxed. Dad welcomed into the house a young British woman named Jill, who moved around the circle in a bright conversational way before going to the captain and hooking her wrists around his elbow.

"Have you seen the ring?" Mom asked Nat and me, as if there was an overlooked Easter egg in the room, so Jill put her hand out, and we all took a gander.

"Isn't it beautiful?" Mom asked, hand on her heart.

"So when did you get engaged?" I asked, although I was bothered that anyone could get romantic when I myself couldn't.

Jill explained that they became engaged a year ago in London, which led to a long story about how she first met Yeshiwas. I listened with half-interest until I could steal several cookies from the tea tray and retreat to my bedroom. Still in a funk, I lay on the bed with earphones, listening to James Taylor and ignoring Nat as he rummaged for a book. I didn't return to the living room until I heard my folks call "good-bye" and shut the front door. Then I sidled to the fire to grab another cookie.

"Well at least you gave them a way to meet," Dad said as Mom cleared away the teacups.

"I guess," she sighed.

"What's the big deal?" I blurted out. "If they're engaged, they can see each other whenever they want."

Mom frowned.

"No, seriously," I added. "Why do we have to play host?"

"How many Ethiopian soldiers have you seen walking around with English fiancées?" Dad asked.

"Then why did they get engaged?"

They looked at me sternly before launching into the actual story. Apparently, Yeshiwas had gone to London to train as a ship navigator. The government of Hailie Selassie had given him a scholarship with the agreement that he would return for several years of civil service, probably in the merchant marines. Then the emperor was overthrown, and though friends warned Yeshiwas not to come back, he felt obliged.

As soon as he arrived, he realized his mistake, but no one would listen to his assurance that he would repay his scholarships if he was allowed to return to his fiancée in England. Instead, he was stripped of his return ticket and conscripted into the Ethiopian Coast Guard. For over a year, he had been navigating a ship in the Red Sea, trying to protect Ethiopia's supply route as Eritrean rebels waged their war of independence, receiving arms shipments from Arab supporters across the Gulf.

Yeshiwas had just gotten a leave of duty—his first. That's why Jill had flown into Addis. But her pleas for his release fell on deaf ears. Government officials were not in the least bit sympathetic toward a foreign woman who expected to be married to an Ethiopian and share life with him in London. So, as it turned out, she had to climb onto a return flight weeping, and the captain had to go back to his ship in the Red Sea. He was forced to continue a high-stakes bluff, hiding his Christian faith and his continued love for a white woman from an imperialist nation.

That night in Addis, I could feel for the two torn lovers, reminded again of my own separation from Nancy. It forced me to see that things could be worse. It also forced me to face the inevitability of what was about to happen in a smaller, less dramatic way—the dreaded event I had been pushing out of my mind for over a month. Finally, a call came from Nancy, who had arrived in Addis and was at the Presbyterian guesthouse with her parents. I was elated but full of despair at the same time, for this call meant I would see Nancy and lose her in almost the same breath.

Forty-Two

Shakespeare's most famous lovers try to reach across the fiery battle line between two rival groups, silhouetted against the blazing rage of warring factions. They loom large and lovely in that ghastly light, until they burst into flames. And my mother, who was always drawn to the sweeping music of Wagner and the tragic tales of the Brontës, watched the drama of Jill and Yeshiwas with a Romeo-and-Juliet intensity.

I think those new star-crossed lovers were, for her, an icon of sorts—a picture of a pure and innocent love that had bloomed, almost impossibly, in the middle of a bitter war. It was hard to believe they even existed, yet it was wonderfully compelling. Here, in Yeshiwas and Jill, was East meets West, Africa meets Europe, Capulets meet Montagues.

How paradoxical that Jill was from that most imperial of imperial nations: Britain. From the very birthplace of the great African explorers Dr. Livingstone and Henry Morton Stanley, not to mention the mission-founding leaders Rowland Bingham or Charles Studd. And how paradoxical that Yeshiwas was so willing to risk everything, prizing Jill over all the fierce revolutionary rhetoric that should keep them separate. Ethiopian communism had no place for such independent desires, but Yeshiwas was determined to keep their love alive. Not until much later would we realize just how determined he really was, and then we would marvel, awed by his amazing resolve.

By contrast to Yeshiwas, there was me: fifteen years younger, still in the care of my parents, naive and faltering in my faith. And there was Nancy, sweet object of my own desire. Though Nancy and I were not from enemy factions like Jill and Yeshiwas or Romeo and Juliet, we were standing on the same fiery fault line, holding hands and completely clueless. I look back now and have to smile. We were so young, so inexperienced. What did we know of love or the compulsions that attend it? Yet how devastating it was to want Nancy the way I did and to feel her slipping away inevitably, pulled right out of my embrace. How hard to sense that there was nowhere to turn for aid. No rescuing savior here. Not even God, it seemed. Just the two of us and our silent prayers drifting up, up into the sky.

Forty-Three

"I've got to go over there right away," I demanded as soon as Nancy called to announce her arrival in Addis.

"What's the rush?" asked my father.

"As if you don't know."

I rolled my eyes, and he laid off. "All right, we'll go after supper." But I saw him glance at Mom as if telegraphing an unspoken joke.

To go after supper meant driving in the dark, which Dad usually tried to avoid due to nighttime guerrilla activity. I appreciated his willingness to take me, but I wished he had agreed to an earlier trip. I feared he would change his mind.

He stuck to the plan, however. That evening he and I climbed into our little Peugeot station wagon then puttered up the drive. As we approached the front entrance, the zebunya stepped out of his guard booth, coming toward us instead of unlatching the gate. He looked medieval in his hooded cloak, face hidden above the lowered flashlight. Dad rolled the window down, but the man didn't joke in Amharic as usual. Instead he swept the backseat with his light, letting it linger in the trunk area.

I wasn't sure if I had just imagined this extra scrutiny, so I asked Dad about it once we were on the street. He admitted we might have a problem. Mom had told the cook that Nat and I would be traveling to Kenya for school in the coming year. Then the cook had told the other staff, which had started speculation that we might all leave the country. They were asking difficult questions, especially the zebunya. To avoid the sort of lockdown that had happened at other stations— and to protect our own possessions—Dad thought we should probably start to move small boxes of stuff out of the house, taking them to Headquarters bit by bit.

As he suggested this bit of subterfuge, his voice low and confidential in the darkness, I felt both thankful for his willingness to share with me and uncomfortable, not used to my father doing anything devious. I felt keyed-up too, wishing that we weren't leaving the country at all. If we stayed, we wouldn't have to go through such charades.

Dad kept his eyes trained on the part of the road lit by the headlamps, leaning over the steering wheel. The streets were quieter than usual, emptied of the standard daytime stream of pedestrians. The only walkers seemed furtive, moving at a quick clip. Cars seemed furtive too, braking briefly at intersections, then zipping away.

A shot went off—a loud pop that broke the purr of the engine— but Dad didn't look at me or say anything, perhaps operating on the assumption that to notice danger was to invite it closer. For a while he asked me questions about Nancy and her older sister, or about their station at Gambela, but I could tell he wasn't really listening. He did not glance at me or lean back into his seat until he pulled into the driveway of the Presbyterian guesthouse, flickering the high beams. Then he tried to revert to his playful self: "Okay, we aren't staying all night. Even romance has to sleep sometime."

I didn't bother to react as the guard appeared in the opening gap. I was too nervous about the prospect of seeing Nancy and being introduced to her parents. As it turned out, Dad actually recognized them from a past encounter, so there was a burst of surprise as soon as they opened the door to their flat. Then came an awkward pause while Nancy stepped forward with her sister. I realized Dad didn't know which girl was which until Nancy shot her left hand out and pulled me to her side, which caused everyone to grin stupidly.

To my relief, her father suggested, "Why don't you two take a walk? We can have some coffee with Dr. Bascom."

I had feared there would be no privacy—that Nancy and I would be forced into making small talk with everyone watching—so this was a blessed mercy.

"Just bring her back before midnight!" Nancy's dad added as she pulled me down the walkway toward the garden. Although my ears burned, I felt relieved. We had hardly moved away from the lit guest room and rounded the corner, when Nancy swung into my arms. I hugged her tighter than ever, her slender length pressed against me, her cheek warm against my own.

"Did you get my letters?" she whispered.

"Letters? As in plural?"

She sighed. "I sent three."

"Well, all I know is that the one I got said that you didn't get either of the ones I sent!"

She sighed again.

"By the way," I added, "I thought the plan was for you to steal the family car. What took so long?"

She giggled. "The roads were all flooded."

"So borrow your dad's boat."

She leaned back in my arms, smiling gently. Then I stopped teasing and asked if I could kiss her. She nodded, so I did, lingering on her lips, tasting her breath in my mouth, warm and musky.

"So how long before you go?" I asked.

"Three days."

Only three days. Now I was the one to sigh. As I gazed over the walls of the guesthouse, which was on a slope above the city, I felt almost angry at the prettiness of the lights glittering below. With the city's battered features hidden, those sparks of brightness seemed too crisp and clean to allow for all the secret violence that was being acted out. They mocked the turmoil that was forcing us apart.

"Have your folks talked any more about coming back?"

She shook her head. "Gambela's out of the picture anyway. The mission's closing it."

"Crap," was all I could muster, which made her poke me in the ribs.

"C'mon, dross lidge," she said, mimicking Dan Coleman's drawl. And though I was reluctant to let go of what I felt, I did. I tried to act like tomorrow didn't exist and we could simply enjoy this moment. I tried to be her happy boyfriend, glad to have a few hours of reunion even if our parents were in the guesthouse talking about a future that would not allow us to see each other.

We had no jackets, and the high altitude air was chilly, so the two of us huddled together on the steps in the garden, looking over the wall to the flickering city below. We joked about the crackle of automatic-weapon fire, imagining that this was Ethiopia's Fourth of July, a dark celebration of independence. Then we kissed and kissed again, tasting each other's longing on our tongues.

In the car on the way back to the CD House, Dad spoke after a long silence. "So the Reynolds seem like nice folks."

"Yeah."

"How's Nancy doing?"

"Okay."

"And what about you?"

I couldn't answer that question. I knew he was reaching for me, trying to be sensitive, but I couldn't confide in him. What did he want me to say? "Yeah, I feel great, except when I get the sensation that I'm walking toward an execution?"

"Well, maybe we can get the two of you together once more."

I groaned as if his attempt to comfort me was a mockery, almost a punishment, which is what I felt at the moment, since he and Mom and Nancy's parents were the ones who were deciding to leave Ethiopia and tear us apart.

"You know," he murmured, "I was once sixteen."

"What's that supposed to mean?"

"I mean I was sixteen, too."

He let me sit with that statement, forced to realize that he had not always been a father or husband—that once he had probably kissed some girl who was not my mother. It was frightening to consider, but it had the effect he was after, causing me to recognize that he wasn't the enemy, at least not in any intentional way.

The next morning when I asked to see Nancy again, I asked in a less demanding manner and Dad made no jokes. He helped to shuttle her across Addis to the CD House so that the two of us could have a full afternoon. We spent most of that time hidden away on the cement verandah behind the main building. Our kisses became hungry, as if we could swallow each other. My hands became hungry, too, sliding up her flanks and grazing the bottom of her breasts.

But there was no satisfaction to be had. The impending fate of our relationship made every caress and kiss seem wrong, as if the two of us were lying over and over, trying to keep something alive that was already dead. The more we touched, the farther apart we seemed. The very passing of time became a kind of taunt whispering in my ear: "There is no future here—no hope at all."

At one point, a servant girl stepped out of the next house, just across the wall, and she tossed a pail of water onto the lawn then grinned at our startled expressions, which added to the sense that we were doing something illicit. I pulled back, looking into Nancy's eyes and seeing my hopelessness mirrored. I was almost relieved to hear my mother call from the front of the building. "Tim? Nancy? Are you two out there? It's time for dinner."

Later that night, after Dad and I drove Nancy back to the Presbyterian guesthouse and her parents came to the car to say a final good-bye, I hugged her listlessly, almost unable to act out the expected tenderness. It was all over now. The two of us had agreed that I would not come to the airport since we had said our good-byes already, breathing them into each other with each anguished kiss.

Nevertheless, the next morning when I woke and realized that the hour was nearing for her flight, I disappeared onto the verandah where we had huddled the day before. Another rainfall had passed and the sun was out momentarily, making droplets glisten. Doves were burbling in the pines. I sat in the middle of it all, numb, simply waiting for one dreaded sound. Every northbound flight passed overhead, so I knew that when I heard a rising drone—and when it rose to a roar—Nancy would be truly leaving.

High above me, a rigid silver jet appeared, ripping across the sky with contrails streaming. As it made its inexorable departure, it left a hard white line straight as a ruler's edge. Only after it disappeared over the shaggy pines did I become aware of a fierce burning in my throat. Heat oozed from my eyes and a hot wind rushed through the hollow of my chest.

Ashes, Ashes . . .

They will raise their voice and cry bitterly over you;
They will sprinkle dust on their heads and roll in ashes.

EZEKIEL 27.30

Forty-Four

F or the next week or two, I moved through each day in a kind of catatonic numbness, hardly aware of anything but my empty core. I never knew that a body could hold so much emptiness.

I watched listlessly as my mother packed little boxes of possessions, surreptitiously slipping them into the Peugeot station wagon with each trip to Headquarters. She would slide these boxes into the footwells or lower individual items into the cargo area and drape a beach towel over them: A stack of Louis L'Amour novels. A portable typewriter. A plaque that hung in the kitchen decorated with hearts—"No matter what, no matter where, it's always home if love is there."

The eyes of the zebunya settled on this draped towel, but he didn't ask to see under it. He just waved us through, mouth set sourly.

I didn't care. I was bitter, too.

I had been in Ethiopia for seven months. That's all. Just long enough to make friends and fall in love and feel like I was part of something much bigger than myself. And now all of it was being stolen away. As a result, I didn't share any of the desire to protect the silly stack of goods accumulating in the basement of the mission guesthouse, squeezed in next to the abandoned property of other fleeing missionaries.

The dissolution of my world felt complete when Mr. Cumbers told my parents that the government was forcing him to close the Community Development House. It had been nationalized, seized from the coffee magnate who rented it to us. For us to stay, the mission would have to pay double rent, which was the government's way of saying that we, as foreign imperialists, were not wanted.

The day my mother announced the closure to the compound staff, explaining that everyone must vacate, the cook wept. "Gaeta," she wailed, "where will I work? How will I feed my family?"

The community development workers were stunned as well, since this had been their one safe haven—a badly needed rest between stints in the famine camps. They packed their few belongings and hugged each other, waving a sad good-bye before scattering to the handful of guesthouses that still existed around Addis. At the gate, they were harassed by the zebunya, now openly belligerent, who wanted to look in each of their bags to make sure they were taking only personal belongings.

"All bedding belongs to the Ethiopian people," he said.

"Not this sleeping bag," replied Tekola. "It has always been mine. Besides, I am part of the Ethiopian people, so it belongs to me twice!" And he walked away.

When at last the main building lay vacant, I wandered over, conscious of the zebunya watching from the gate. Inside the tall glass-paned doors, I took a slow tour, saddened by the echoing of the rooms. Though the building had been stripped clean, it felt full of ghosts. I was aware of all the erasures that were occurring—of the coffee tycoon who had lost his fortune, of the laughing Irish woman and her lover, of eloquent Solomon debunking Marxism while everyone shouted "Amen," of fierce Tekola who had challenged me to eat with my right hand, of Nancy smiling wistfully on the stone verandah.

Thirty years later my parents would receive an email from Tekola, who wanted to know if they were the same people he had known so long ago. He would explain that he had tried repeatedly to gain entrance to a veterinary school outside Ethiopia, and when he was granted permission to go to Japan, he never returned, instead marrying a Japanese woman. Another of the residents, a tall elegant woman named Sehin, would contact my parents by phone, explaining that she was living in the United States and struggling to make ends meet as a fashion model. Solomon Abate would show up in Chicago, living in an apartment with four Vietnamese refugees who lay their mattresses on the floor, creating a wall-to-wall bed that smelled of old socks and garlic. He would talk nonstop about his lost library, convinced that if he just had his books again, he could stage a comeback as a guest speaker or evangelist or prophet without a country. A little

more study and he could make it back to Africa to be reconciled with
his lost wife and children.

Such a long, long drift! And so much taken away! Somehow as I
walked through the high-ceilinged rooms of the CD House, I could
already feel the terrible space opening up between us all. When I
paused by the tall windows with their gauzy drapes, I felt as if I stood
in a museum exhibit where everything had been reduced to placards:
here is where they ate, here is where they slept, here is where they
once thought they were sheltered and would stay together and not be
dragged away to separate fates.

A few dirty pots were piled in the kitchen sink. A few pieces of
weary furniture were shoved into corners. Everything else was bare
stone and glass, cold and blank. And I realized as I looked around that
I wanted to take something that might stand as a memento, even a
small reminder that I had actually lived here.

All I could find was an ostrich egg in the room that had served
as a common lounge. It was displayed in a gilded filigree bowl, and
it seemed a fitting symbol. Slightly yellowed, pitted lightly, it was a
closed shell, hard as abalone—a hope that hadn't hatched.

I lifted the egg off its stand and slipped it into my shirt before
walking out as casually as possible, arms crossed so that the zebunya
wouldn't see my bulge. Later, that egg would go into our car under
the loot-hiding beach towel. It would go into a box at the mission
headquarters, along with a leather biker jacket I had scavenged from
another family's barrel. It would eventually travel to Kenya and Sudan
and then Iowa, where it still resides on a desk, whispering its singular
message: "Remember, remember."

I slept fitfully during the last few nights at the CD compound. Mom
and Dad had received confirmation that they would be redeployed,
probably to Sudan. Although it might take months to secure the necessary visas, they were going to fly out of the country with Nat and
me to wait for clearance in Kenya. They had bought the plane tickets,
and we would leave a week after shifting over to Headquarters.

As I lay there in my bed at the CD place, I was conscious not just

of the empty building across the lawn but all the other empty buildings that had gone with my life in Ethiopia. I was conscious of the
large compound that had once been Good Shepherd Academy, where
the classrooms stood empty now, waiting to be converted into hospital wards for wounded veterans back from the wars in Eritrea and
Somalia. I was conscious of the padlocked house on the mountain
near Bulki. The silent house where Nancy had once lived in Gambela.
All the vacated schools and hospitals and homes at stations that had
been occupied by friends like the Colemans and Iwans and Dyes. I
was conscious, too, of the empty pharmacy that Waja once ran, and
the churches in southern Ethiopia with doors nailed shut. Also of
the distraught cook who had no income now, and the unhappy guard
hunched in his little gate-closet, trying to find motivation to stand
up and walk the fence line. Was he out there right now, staring at the
side of our house, feeling divided between his better instincts and angry resentment? Was he mulling over the advice of some local kebele
member who had insisted, most likely, that he harass us at each stage
of our departure?

My brother Nat, on the bunk bed above me, had slipped into sleep
as easily as ever. I was envious. I listened to his smooth breathing until
I dozed. Then I jerked awake, having imagined that I heard something,
a faint crunching as if someone was settling a foot on cornflakes. But
no, this sound wasn't imagined. I heard it again, miniscule yet distinct,
and I surfaced out of my stupor, realizing that someone was creeping
up the cement steps next to our little sunporch bedroom.

Those outdoor steps, which were never used, led to a locked door
right beside my bed. And I happened to know that a light bulb had
broken out there, scattering bits of powdered glass. I knew because I
had come across shards of that broken bulb while shooting my slingshot at birds across the stream.

I tensed in my blankets. Now that I could hear nothing, I assumed
the interloper was standing only inches away, screened by the curtains
Mom had hung. Could this be the zebunya on his rounds, pausing
for some mysterious reason? If not, then thieves? Or worse, a death
squad?

With a muffled crack, one of the windows in the door shattered
and glass scattered across my blanket, sending me into panicked
prayer: "Lord, please, please, please."

I tensed for gunfire, squeezing my eyelids so hard that I saw flickering lights. For a moment, I was absolutely incapable of reaction, rendered helpless. The silence of the moment was more ominous than the cracking glass itself, since it was pregnant with sinister possibilities. I swallowed a desire to scream. I swallowed my breath itself. Somehow Nat was still asleep, and I could hear his calm inhalations, which made me resolve that I had to do something. If there was a gun out there, the two of us were right next to it. Soon the assailant would realize this. So I lifted the blankets slightly and rolled onto the floor, quiet as a cat.

After the briefest pause, I bear-walked into the hallway then scuttled to my parents' room.

"Dad. Mom. There's someone breaking in."

"What?"

My father, who always wakened with difficulty, lifted himself on an elbow and rubbed at his brow, but Mom sprang out of bed. She glided to the door and started down the hall. The two of us arrived at my bedroom just as a hand appeared in the shadows of the curtains, reaching through the broken window between upper and lower bunk so as to finger the doorknob.

This surreptitious movement suggested to me, for the first time, that the intruder was a thief, not a military thug. Then came a surge of rage. I wanted to grab the secretive hand and saw it across the jagged glass. I lunged forward. But before I could cross the room, Mom screamed and pandemonium took over. The hand flew back. There was crunching on the cement steps. Nat sat up, asking, "What, what?" And Dad shouted from the hall, "Everyone stay put."

I wasn't going to stay, though. I lifted my slingshot from the bedside table and ran for the front door. I was sick of fear itself, outraged by the way that it had preyed on me. I wanted to chase this bogey monster down and knock him to the ground.

When I stepped out into the dark, I couldn't see the zebunya's flashlight even though Mom's screams should have alerted him. I bellowed, "Leba," the Amharic term for "thief," then saw a light flicker. But before the guard could jog down the lawn, I was off again, dashing to the opposite corner of the house, trying to trap the fleeing intruder, to pin him against the fence. As I ran, I scooped up a handful of gravel and fitted a pebble into the pouch of my slingshot.

Dad called out, "Tim, get back here," but I ignored him and ducked into the shadows, high-stepping in my bare feet to avoid rocks and shrubs.

Crouched by the darkened wall, I held my breath and began to think more clearly. Even if I could hit this guy with a rock, I would have no other defense. What if he had a knife or gun?

I was relieved when the zebunya's light grew brighter behind the house and he stepped into view. He turned the beam toward me and grunted. He muttered a sentence in Amharic, including the word *yellem*, which meant he had come up empty-handed. Then he moved away, searching farther down the fence.

For a moment, I thought about following him, but decided to stay. I knew that by now the guard was just carrying out his standard protocol. Nat came out onto the tarmac, too, and discovered that our car was broken into. As he and Dad huddled at the door, checking the glove compartment, I asked if the thief had gotten anything.

"Yep," Dad replied, turning with an odd grin. "He's now the proud owner of about a hundred gospel tracts."

"You think he'll become a Christian?" Nat asked.

"Maybe. In fact, maybe we've started a whole new ministry. The Leba ministry."

I knew they were attempting to defuse the panic. They joked about how the thief would react when he had enough light to realize he had stolen tracts, not a stack of Ethiopian bills. I smirked, trying to enjoy the thought, but I felt conscious that there was nothing very funny about this situation. We were at risk now more than ever, since there was no one else living in the compound. I was suspicious, too, about the zebunya, wondering whether he could be trusted. Did he even care what happened to us? For that matter, could he have been in cahoots with this thief? Is that why he was so slow to respond?

The next day I woke jumpy and exhausted, ready to help pack the final suitcases—to get into the station wagon and drive to the gate, leaving for the last time. My desire to stay and stick it out was broken. At our mission headquarters, at least the wall would be higher and made of stone.

On the way out, however, we had to stop for the guard one last time. Instead of unlatching the gate, he came to the car, glancing toward the rear compartment as Dad asked about last night's burglar. Back there, our final suitcases and boxes were stacked, and the zebunya kept eyeing them as he grunted replies or pointed toward an apparent rip in the fence. He pursed his lips, dropping eye contact as he launched into a longer statement, and that is when I noticed Dad's jaw muscles rippling.

My father wedged in a reply, but the guard went right back into his lengthy declaration, talking more loudly and uttering the nationalistic slogan, "Etiopia tikdem." Without another glance, he turned and went to the back of the car, where he opened the back hatch to lift out our suitcases.

"What's he doing?" Nat demanded, reaching for his door handle, but Dad cautioned him to stay put. "Be patient," he said. "Things will be okay."

"Not if we don't have anything to wear."

"Trust me. There's nothing we can do until we've talked with Mr. Cumbers."

I was beyond caring—too beaten down to react—so I didn't have anything to add, not even after we got out on the road and Dad gave us the expected story: that the zebunya had claimed everything for the Ethiopian government.

"He said we could take nothing except ourselves," Dad explained. "'What about the Holy Spirit?' That's what I asked. 'Is the government going to keep the Holy Spirit, because I am hoping to take the Spirit with me.'"

"You didn't!" Mom interjected, and Nat grinned, looking at me to see whether I appreciated our father's comeback.

"He can have it all," I muttered. "Who cares?"

Then, after a moment of silence, Mom sighed. "It could be worse, you know? At least we're not in jail like Waja or Dr. Cannata."

Forty-Five

M y father may have joked about the government confiscating the Holy Spirit from us, but at the time, that's exactly how it felt—as if the zebunya had lifted God right out of the hatch of our station wagon to padlock with our suitcases!

Of course, I didn't dare acknowledge that feeling—not back then, as a teenager. To acknowledge such doubt was tantamount to betraying God. All things work together for good, the apostle Paul had insisted, but only for those who love God, and how can you love God if you feel God is absent? No, if I started to doubt, things would certainly NOT work together for good, and where would that leave me? Whirling into the sky like a spark about to fizzle?

So I tried to soldier on, empty and cold but clinging desperately to the very need to believe. I went on trying, trying, trying, to somehow breathe life back into the ashes, down there where I might find an ember of faith remaining, no matter how small it might be. A single spark, we used to sing, that's all it takes to start a fire.

In retrospect, having surveyed the five decades of my life, it's clear that this core dilemma has always been with me—this deep personal struggle to believe, which makes me wonder if some people are simply given the ability to believe and some are not. "Given," that is, in the sense that they are given blonde hair or brunette, eagle eyes or blind. In my case, ever since birth I had been the child who saw what was wrong with the picture. Puddleglum, my mother called me. Or sometimes Eeyore. My brothers, inheritors of the same history, were not geared so negatively. Johnathan had purpose—enough to overcome whatever obstacles he felt. Nat had natural sunniness, enough to rise out of gloom. Me? I always felt doubt, even as young as six or seven, when my mother asked me what I wanted to be some day and I said "a bum."

Such resignation was simply wrong in the missionary world. The appropriate response to difficulty was a positive, anything-is-possible attitude, and so the "aunts" and "uncles" that I inherited there arose confidently, sure that each new day would bring something good. They even relished conflict, convinced that God, when put to the test, would come to their aid.

How I wished I felt the same way! When I woke to a new day, especially a difficult one, it didn't look so promising. I questioned what good could emerge out of rotten circumstances. I found myself irritable and resistant. I became especially reactive if others claimed certainty about what God wanted. "It must be God's will," they asserted, but I had a hard time accepting that word "must."

I still can't help this response; skepticism sweeps over me when people seem to have an unwarranted conviction about what God wants—what exactly is God's desire or plan. I feel mean-spirited to critique such optimistic, purposeful people (some of whom have showed me an unwarranted degree of patience and love), but I can't help it. For all of my youth, I read the scriptures and prayed and listened for a whisper of a response no matter how small it might be: a verse that seemed uncannily apt, an unexpected opportunity that suggested a new direction, a mysterious flicker of joy, any odd synchronicity of events that might serve as a "sign." Like a water dowser with a divining rod, I walked the fields back and forth, waiting for the magic dip and tug, though it remained ever elusive. Since I did not experience clear assurance, I continue to doubt when others act convinced by their own special revelation. Unable to block my innate skepticism (just like they are unable to block their innate positivism), I hedge my bets.

Forty-Six

During that last week in Ethiopia, at the heart of July, it seemed the rains would not let up. The downpour was endless. Thick gray clouds pressed down over the mountain-slope city, dulling the ranks of galvanized rooftops. They released their wet loads in a torrent—a cascade so heavy and constant that every building became a kind of thundering drum, every auto a sounding box. On the roadside, pedestrians hoisted umbrellas and disappeared into closets of streaming water, or they ran, stutter-step, leaping puddles as they carried cardboard shields overhead. When they found shelter under a shop awning, they leaned despondently against the damp walls, all progress cut off by the fickle tyranny of the skies.

Nat and I rode through those wet streets on errands with Dad. We rode along on the morning he was allowed to reclaim our suitcases from the storage shed where the zebunya had locked them. We also rode along when he posted a set of letters to friends in America, asking for prayer as we transitioned out of Ethiopia. We went for the sheer relief of seeing something outside the four closed walls of our room or the cramped corridor that led down to the dining hall and its alcove of musty religious novels.

One afternoon at the end of that long week, with clouds pressing down so thick it seemed like night, we rode shotgun as my father drove to the Ethiopian Airlines office, where he would confirm our flight to Nairobi. A light drizzle had turned into a waterfall, shattering off the windshield in a surf that came and went with each swipe of the wipers. As those blades swept back and forth, we saw snatches of traffic and people leaping with jackets over their hunched heads. It was a kind of peekaboo world that made most cars slow down, but Dad kept clipping along, trying to get to the offices before they closed. Not sure if he had missed a turn, he glanced to his right just as a crouched figure jumped the gutter on our left.

This unexpected pedestrian dashed across the oncoming lane. She was a woman of the poorest sort—her cotton skirt and shawl stained gray except where they were turned black by the rain. She had the shawl up over her head, which meant she could not see anything except what was right in front of her. Worse, there was a hump on her back, outlined under the wet cloth—no doubt a baby.

"Watch out!" I yelled, and my father, who was completely blind in his left eye, stomped on the brake, swinging his head to see what was the matter.

The woman kept her pace, not lifting her head as she loped into our lane, so Dad had only one option—swerving into the opposite lane in hopes that she might clear the front of the car. It seemed for an instant that she might outrun us. If she had been at all aware, she could have jumped free. However, she stayed at the same steady pace and our right headlamp caught her with a fateful thump, flipping her onto the hood, where she tumbled and dropped away.

Thunk-a-thunk. That's how fast it happened. Then there was just the squeal of brakes.

My father leaped out, leaving the door open in the rain. I stepped out more cautiously, afraid to see whatever we were going to see. And Nat followed.

By the time I reached Dad and the woman, she was already trying to stand despite his efforts to keep her still. He wanted to protect broken bones, but she was desperate to get out of the road. As a result, he felt forced to help her stagger to the curb, where she sat down groaning. Then I heard the baby squall on her back and felt a mixture of distress and relief. Alive, yes, but how badly hurt?

My father kept apologizing—"Awzunalow." He asked her a question in Amharic, to which she only shook her head. I was so fixated on her wincing face that I did not notice the people who had stepped out from under the eaves of a shop—not until I sensed their half circle at our backs and glanced up, alarmed by furrowed brows and acid gazes.

Dad asked the injured woman something in Amharic again, gesturing to our car as if to say, "Can we pick you up and take you? Can we drive you to the hospital?"

She shrank away, and a man in the crowd muttered in a tone unmistakably accusatory.

"Awo," murmured several of the bystanders, nodding with heavy frowns, and I heard a passing youth call out in English, "Hey, you! Is this what you do to our people?"

There was only one person in this growing crowd who had actually knelt down to help. When I looked more closely I realized, to my surprise, that I recognized him. It was one of the relief workers we had hosted at the Community Development House—a quiet thoughtful man named Getachew, who had never made much of an impression on me, not engaging in the usual dining-room banter. He leaned forward now, listening to whatever the woman was trying to say through her clenched teeth.

"She says it is hurting here," Getachew said, pointing at her right hip. Then, under his breath, he added, "But, doctor, you must go."

My father didn't look at him, despite shaking his head.

Still, Getachew was adamant. "No, it is too much dangerous. You must go. Take the boys. I can help."

Dad locked eyes with him at last, grimacing. I knew how terrible this decision was. I could see it written on his face like a sudden nausea. He had spent not just the last eight months, but five other years of his life, trying to save injured people like this—the most helpless of the helpless. As a Christian, it was his duty. Plus, this time the damage was his own fault. Why should the young worker from the CD House stay to take the consequences?

A pair of tall, suit-coated men had stopped under their umbrellas, and they started to talk in an animated way, causing the others to nod.

The youth with the English words was standing next to them, and he threw out another taunt. "Hey, my friend, is this what they teach in America?"

"Dad," I said, pulling at his sleeve. "We've got to go."

Finally my father stood. This conscientious doctor—a determined Christian who had debated openly with gun-toting soldiers—stood up, convinced by the fear in my voice. What justice could he expect if the crowd took over? And what might happen to his sons?

The woman had just untied the wrap on her back to bring her baby forward. For a moment, it stopped squalling and blinked at the raindrops on its forehead, which caused everyone to fall silent. In that pause, Dad pulled out his wallet, handing all the bills to Getachew. "Please give her this," he said. Then he turned away.

As we quick-walked toward the car, I could hear Getachew speaking to the crowd in loud Amharic, asking a pointed question. I knew he was trying to distract them.

The youth with the English comments made one last attempt to create a scene. "Hey, where ar-ra you going?" But the crowd was not focused enough to follow his cue.

We stepped back into the car and drove away.

Still, to this day, I have not spoken with my father or my brother about that incident on the rainy street in Addis, yet I'm sure that it glowers in their memories as it does in mine, tinged with a kind of yellow shame. "You must go," said our Ethiopian friend. "I can take care of her." So we walked away. And a few days later, we walked away again, down the hallways of the Addis airport to our boarding gate, leaving the troubles of Ethiopia for the people who remained.

Just as when we arrived, the airport hallways were guarded by soldiers in olive uniforms and black boots, with machine guns slung from their shoulders. The same bored, irritable men stared at us with the same sullen eyes, waiting for an excuse to exercise their brute power. However, this time I had the fear that an officer might step forward, calling out our names, then take us into custody for our secret crime against the masses—symbolized by the battered woman on the curb.

"You missionaries!" he would say. "Look what you have done! You claim to be helping our people, but look at the one you have destroyed. Do you think you are immune? That you can just walk away?"

When finally we were buckled in and the plane lifted off, I felt a sad relief looking down at the wet streets and the dull gray rooftops with their blackened stovepipes and flumes of smoke. I was conscious of all those who could not leave like us. Kind and brave people like Getachew. Like Joseph, the dresser at Bulki. Or Waja, still in some prison memorizing pages from a torn-up Bible. I thought of cool Yared, too, who had protected me every day on the bus to Good Shepherd but was now out of a job. Would I ever see him again? Then we rose into the clouds and there was nothing to see out the window except gray.

A Voice from the Flames

Moses saw that though the bush was on fire it did not burn up. So Moses thought, "I will go over and see this strange sight—why the bush does not burn up."

When the LORD saw that he had gone over to look, God called to him from within the bush, "Moses! Moses!"

And Moses said, "Here I am."

"Do not come any closer," God said. "Take off your sandals, for the place where you are standing is holy ground."

EXODUS 3.2 — 5

Forty-Seven

O nly once more would I get near to Ethiopia before leaving the continent of Africa. And then I would stand just close enough to realize how far away I had come.

By the middle of my senior year at Rift Valley Academy, my parents had moved to Sudan to work at a village only thirty miles from the Ethiopian border. There, my father was trying to resurrect a hospital abandoned during the civil war of the sixties. My older brother Johnathan had left college and come to live with them, having undergone some undisclosed crisis, the sort of crisis that I would only start to understand after I myself was in college and experienced panic attacks triggered by something as slight as dorm mates shouting good-bye down the hall.

In any case, Johnathan had traveled to Khartoum with our father to meet Nat and me when we flew in from Kenya. It was strange to see him shrunk by the three inches I had added since we last saw each other. A tangled afro and goatee disguised his features. However, once I recognized him, I was swept by memories of the life we had once known in Kansas, where I had—so long ago it seemed—felt restless enough and idealistic enough to volunteer for this heart-splitting tour of duty.

How far away Troy now seemed, from where I got only an occasional letter describing how the football team had almost reached the state championship and how a third of the girls in our class had become pregnant. Would I have made a difference in that final game? Would I have contributed to the list of pregnancies? It was hard to imagine any of it now, having followed such a different path.

Although I was glad to have Johnathan back, I was also jealous that he had taken over as the eldest son, speaking Arabic and seeming to be a close confidant to my father. Since there was no missionary plane available for our return to the new station in the south, the two of them consulted and decided we should travel atop a rented Bedford truck loaded with medical supplies. For the next two days and nights we jolted slowly toward the Ethiopian border, weaving through dunes then scrub brush, often brought to a crawl by a maze of rutted trails. The farther we went, the more we had to fight for room on this truck, since the surly driver added paying passengers. Eventually, fifteen of us were bumping along, elbow to elbow in the blazing wind, falling silent for whole hours as our eyes dried shut.

I was not the same sixteen-year-old who had left Ethiopia a year and a half earlier, shattered emotionally but trying to emulate the vibrant faith I had seen in members of the persecuted church. At Rift Valley Academy, I had become disillusioned by what seemed a shadow version of Christianity. Chapel sessions and daily Bible class called for a kind of compulsory spirituality, performed as mere routine. My own devotions were a dry habit. I forced them upon myself like the mandatory devotions at Bingham Academy, only now there was none of the surrounding urgency of war, not enough exterior tension to kickstart my interior life. And when I visited the family of one of my new classmates on the edge of Nairobi, that cooled my ardor further. I felt like a sham, lolling around on shag carpet and playing Monopoly, or hitting golf balls at an elite British club where they had a membership. This was taking up one's cross and following Jesus?!

Sudan, at least, did not offer such guilt-inducing comforts. I remember, for instance, that on our truck trip to the south, I spent an entirely sleepless night on the concrete floor of a fueling station, tortured by hot, still air and droning mosquitoes. Then I spent a second day rocking under the blazing sun, muscles screaming as I had to duck under low-lying thorn trees.

A second night came and we still had not arrived. After several hours of steering through the dark, the driver turned off the engine in the wide-open blackness, where not a light could be seen, not even the yellow flicker of a peasant fire. He told everyone to sleep where they were, and we obeyed, curling body to body, too tired to care about the close stench of sweat. My brother Nat fell off the truck at one point, slamming down on his side, then just clambered back aboard and drifted to sleep.

It was all becoming surreal—like a kind of endless hallucination.

Before the sun rose, we woke to engine noise and the grinding of gears. I grabbed for the slatted truck siding, struggling to remember where I was. I felt I might still be dreaming as I stared down the dawn corridor of the road and saw what appeared to be a huge pale ball dangling from the arm of a baobab. It got bigger and bigger, until it burst against the back of a dozing woman, poofing out over all the passengers. Everyone laughed—even the stunned woman—as we realized the ball was a bale of straw hoisted out of reach from passing animals. I laughed too. It was all so utterly fantastic—the long-limbed oil-black people, the throaty Arabic shouts, the bulging trunks of the baobabs—that I wasn't sure I could believe my senses. Was any of it real?

I was still in this out-of-body state four hours later when we arrived at our destination and I saw my mother running toward us, scattering a cluster of startled pigs. She seemed to be another player in our little theater of the absurd, dashing from a mud-walled house in a long floral dress that fluttered red and yellow and green. I smiled as she gave me a hug, though I was too worn out to register her touch. Then I followed her into the adobe house, where I stumbled down a hallway, fell onto a cot, and slept for fourteen hours straight, oblivious to the pigs that had returned, grunting, into the shade along the eaves.

Ethiopia had felt politically hostile, threatening us with daily violence, but Sudan was even more difficult in terms of sheer physical survival. Every day when I woke, I pined for the cool, thin air of the Ethiopian highlands. At our new station in the flat-baked scrub brush of the desert, midday temperatures peaked over 110 degrees Fahrenheit. Waves of heat, carried by the wind, seemed to pierce everything. Dust whirled through the screens. In the burnt ruin of the afternoon, every living thing gave up and took shelter—even the scorpions that crept into cracks or the bats that dangled from our rafters, panting.

This was not an easy place to live, and there was a stark reminder of our own fragile mortality not far from the house, in a tiny fenced lot where two cement gravestones marked the resting places of missionaries who had died in the 1940s, colleagues of Malcolm Forsberg, my parents' mentor at candidate school. After Malcolm was forced out of Bulki station by the invading Italians, he ended up here in Sudan. Then the Italians sent bombers over the Ethiopian border to conduct a surprise aerial raid, and two of his colleagues were hit as they ran from their house. He had rushed down from a nearby station where he was working, arriving only in time to help dig the graves.

This somber reminder of nearby Ethiopia caused it to crop up again in our conversations. We swooped to it like the moths around our dinner lamp, singeing our wings. And one of those twilight evenings, as my parents passed on news about some of the people who had fled Mengistu's regime, they brought up a forgotten character. They said that while they were getting oriented in Khartoum, they were surprised by a ghostly visitor at the mission headquarters. A tall, gaunt man in a flowing *jellabia* had come asking for them, and when he threw back the cloth over his head, they instantly recognized him, though they struggled to remember how. Two years had passed, and he was no longer in his khaki uniform. Not until he gave them his name did they realize that they were staring at a worn-out version of Yeshiwas, the Ethiopian naval officer who had been conscripted and forced to serve on a ship in the Red Sea.

Mom said she wept to see how much the man had aged. His hair had thinned and his cheeks were sunken from hunger, although he had the same gracious, soft-spoken manner. A year ago, he explained, he had fled Addis Ababa during a military leave, determined to finally escape to his fiancée. After walking hundreds of miles in the disguise of a peasant, he crossed the border into Sudan, got forced into a refugee camp, and after months of frustrating negotiation, was permitted to travel to Khartoum. He still did not know, however, if he would be allowed out of the country, despite contacting Jill in London and getting her to write letters to the Sudanese authorities.

Of course, when Mom described the continued suffering of this couple, it set off echoes of my own lost love. Looking at a map did not help, since I realized that Nancy's former home was just south of Doro, across the border, probably reachable in a few hours of driving. While I knew there was nothing there to give me solace, I longed instinctively to get closer, until at last I had an actual opportunity. Dad announced that he needed to immunize children in a village near the border, and I agreed to be his assistant.

On the scheduled morning, the two of us borrowed the station's only vehicle, a battered Land Rover, to travel twenty or thirty miles closer to the border. I enjoyed the way the terrain lifted as we went, then how it began to wrinkle with gullies and humps. I enjoyed the way that the houses along the dirt trail were similar to Ethiopian homes—small round adobe huts with conical thatch roofs—except brighter because of the way they were decorated with swirling patterns of white paint. It seemed to me that perhaps these houses were not so different than those of the Anuak or Nuer people on the other side of the border, where Nancy had lived.

My father stopped at last beside a cluster of huts, explaining to a bowed and wrinkled man, through broken Arabic, that we would like to give shots to the children of this area so that we could protect them from future illnesses. The old man went limping from hut to hut, alerting mothers, then shuffled off into the brush, hollering his hoarse message. Women slowly gathered, stooping out of huts or strolling from the forest, carrying babies and naked toddlers. One child broke loose to run back into the scraggly woods, which made all the mothers laugh, gangly and gap-toothed due to the custom of removing two bottom incisors as a beauty mark.

At this time, Dad gave me a quick lesson on how to use the immunization gun so that he could focus on examining children and prescribing medicines. With the canister of serum locked in place, all I had to do was disinfect the arm with alcohol, then press the trigger. The correct dose would squirt into the skin.

Most kids, despite their fear, came forward and walked away fine, relieved to have survived this contact with a foreigner and his strange tool. A few cried, rubbing at the weeping pinprick. But the one who haunted me was a baby that made no movement at all.

"Dad, what should I do with this one?" I called, as the mother brought her listless child out of a cloth sling. After she unwrapped him, I flinched. He was a skeleton with skin.

My father pinched and lifted a bit of flesh. When he released, it stayed lifted. "Completely dehydrated," he said. "I doubt this baby will live more than a day or two."

He tried to get a bit more information from the mother, ushering her away from the line, but she shook her head and planted her feet. She held the baby toward me. At last Dad relented, saying, "It can't hurt, I guess."

The baby's arm was so emaciated that I was afraid I'd hit bone. I lifted a fold of skin like my dad had done, just so I would have something to work with. Then I pulled the trigger.

The baby opened his mouth wide, skin taut on his skull, but no sound came out. Never had I seen death so close and merciless. Not even when I passed the boy with the bullet hole in his head, lying outside an Addis school. Here it was still at work, and it was happening to someone who so clearly should be exempt. The gun in my hand was supposed to bring healing, but I couldn't help thinking of it as an executioner's weapon.

What else could I do but pull the trigger and swallow my feelings and keep on treating the other children, relieved that they, at least, jerked their arms away. I was just glad when the line ended and none was left to look at me in dread. We packed the equipment into the Land Rover and climbed in for the return trip. Then, instead of turning back toward Doro, Dad surprised me by proposing that we drive a few more miles toward the border.

On we went, down a trail that was not much more than a cow path with a few tire ruts. We slumped into gullies and back out, until at last we topped a small rise and I could see a series of smoky ridges: the mountains beyond the plains of western Ethiopia. There, my father turned off the Land Rover and we got out to look across the vast wilderness with the hot engine ticking at our backs.

"How do you know where the border is?" I asked.

"I don't. We might even be in Ethiopia."

"So what if we just kept driving?"

"Eventually, we'd get in a heap of trouble."

It was January 1979, and Ethiopia was still in the grip of Colonel Mengistu. Though the country had ended its war with Somalia, defeating the U.S.-backed invaders, the war of independence in Eritrea had escalated, with rebels laying siege to the Ethiopian troops who occupied the capital of Asmara. To maintain his military strength, Mengistu had signed a twenty-year accord with the USSR. The Ministry of Labor was hinting that the mission headquarters in Addis would be nationalized now. They were eyeing the compound for Bingham Academy too. The fire was intensifying. So why did I feel such longing as I looked toward those haze-shrouded foothills?

We stood silent for a long time, staring eastward. Then my father suddenly said, "It's a little like looking across the River Jordan, don't you think?"

I nodded, recalling the story of the Israelites gathering at the Jordan after forty years of desert exile. They had wandered for so long that a whole generation died without reaching their hoped-for refuge. Even Moses was blocked at the end, only able to look across the waters to remind his people how the Lord had taken them out of the iron-smelting furnace of Egypt, leading them with a pillar of flame, and how God had spoken to them from the burning mountain of Horeb. "Has any other people heard the voice of God speaking out of fire," he asked, "and lived?"

Communist Ethiopia was no Promised Land, flowing with milk or honey. Quite the contrary. But in some strange way as I stood there in Sudan, unable to turn back time or move forward in space, I felt like I was looking across a great gulf at the place where I belonged. Even though I was less sure of my faith than I had been two years ago when entering Ethiopia, I felt the pull back toward that turbulent place, back to where I had felt most alive spiritually, surrounded by people who were also trying to come to terms with what they believed, or didn't. In my own way, I had heard the voice of God speaking out of fire—and I had lived.

Epilogue

et the tape spin forward thirty-three years, past my return to America and my college graduation, past my wedding and the birth of two sons, past the ouster of Colonel Mengistu and the establishment of a new Federal Democratic Republic, past a hundred of my sons' soccer games and rock concerts. Let the tape spool all the way to December 2010, when I finally step down from a mud-splattered Land Cruiser eight thousand feet in altitude, with rain clouds drifting across the road below me, veiling the snaking tire tracks and the white humpbacked cow.

There I am finally, a fifty-year-old making his long-awaited return. The road before me is no longer passable, petering out in a stand of eucalyptus—big mature trees that I don't recall, which disorients me and makes me wonder if we are even on the right mountain. Then I see a glimmer of tin and start forward, hopscotching slick puddles, red with iron-rich sediment.

Behind me I hear a shouted caution, "Ahbeit, Timotheus, you will fall down I think."

It is Sahle Tilahun who calls to me—my father's old traveling companion—who has kindly come south on this trip, translating at each of the abandoned mission stations where I once lived. We have even passed through Arba Minch, where Sahle and my father snapped the fan belt and had to jury-rig a substitute from Dr. Dina's pantyhose.

"Look at your daddy," I hear him stage-whispering. "He is remembering, I think."

I know without glancing that Sahle has his hand on the shoulder of my eighth-grade son Luke, shepherding him down the same rain-gutted trail, smiling widely, his bronze face lit up by the sheer newness of this place he has never been, his silver hair swept back in a cresting wave. I have brought Luke with me, and Sahle has brought Temesgen, his twenty-five-year-old son, who is newly married and expecting a baby, happy to come to an area famous for its homemade butter, a traditional gift for a pregnant wife.

Temesgen is also editor of a nationally distributed magazine published by the Kale Heywet denomination, the same denomination begun in the 1920s and 1930s by the first Sudan Interior Mission workers, including my parents' mentors, the Forsbergs. How remarkable it is to think that the Forsbergs actually began their newlywed life right here on this very mountain, staying until the mid-1930s, when they were forced into exile by the invading Italians. My parents were only in grade school at that time, but in the eighty years since—in the single lifespan of their generation—that brand-new denomination has gone from a hundred scattered adherents to over five million, mushrooming despite decades of persecution.

Incredible growth it would seem, although not that much more rapid than in other parts of Africa, where at the time of Livingstone and Marx, Christianity hardly existed except as an Orthodox presence in Ethiopia and as a flickering colonial influence at coastal outposts. It's almost mind-boggling to think that, in only 150 years, the African population of Christians has shot up from 1 or 2 percent to more than 40. To think that now there are more than 400 million Christians across the continent—Protestant, Charismatic, Catholic, Orthodox.

I feel a bit like a traitorous double-agent as I weave through the woods, sidestepping puddles. Supposedly I have come on official church business. With the help of Sahle and Temesgen, I have bargained for a vehicle and driver from the headquarters of the Kale Heywet church in Addis, banking on the reputation of my parents as former missionaries. We have made it all the way to this mountain, two days' drive from the capital, because the church administrators imagine me writing an inspirational, edifying tale of my parents' life in Ethiopia and the church's growth. I know they are expecting something in a proselytizing vein, and I have committed a sin of omission by not offering a more candid explanation. So I feel guilty about the thoughts that occur to me about Marxism and missionaries and the hymn of my youth, "Onward Christian Soldiers." I feel a bit guilty, too, about the cheerful Kale Heywet minister who met us this morning and agreed to guide us up the mountain in his bright red Arsenal soccer jacket, willing to drop everything to help an odd stranger.

The trees come to an end, and I stop walking.

"I think he knows it," I hear behind me. "Do you know the place, Timotheus?"

Do I know it? How to answer that? How to even speak when I am swept by such conflicted emotions—the sadness of all the years lost and the deep satisfaction of finally, finally being back where I never wanted to leave?

At my feet, the green bowl-like sweep of the mountain saddle appears just as I recall, confirmed by a ragged square of foundation stones that used to support my father's old clinic. And the familiar twisty trail shoots up the far slope behind that ghostly foundation. More importantly, on the ridge I see what I was afraid to even hope to see. Marvel of marvels, a very familiar low-slung cottage with a stained metal roof and broken windows, with a kind of checkerboard siding of woven bamboo scraped brown under the paint but still there, still whispering, "You didn't dream it all. You really did live here once! And though you thought this place might have been erased, it has been here all along!"

When I finally pivot to answer Sahle, a stranger has appeared alongside him—a gaunt sixty-year-old with stubble and a furrowed brow. He is wearing black rubber boots and a yellowing shamma around his neck.

The minister in the Arsenal warm-up arrives, too, and offers an explanation: "This is the Bulki pastor, Ato Tekle. I told him to come because he is the one living here the longest years."

The newcomer studies his colleague's lips, brow wrinkling as if concentrating on a difficult equation. Then he gazes at me shyly. Although I want to turn and run toward my house, I hold out my hand. "Tenahstehlin. It is good to meet you. I am Timotheus."

A warm smile cracks the fixity of this man's worn face. He nods, stepping forward and bowing, gripping himself at the wrist as if offering the right hand as a detachable gift.

"You can ask him questions," the Arsenal minister says in a cheerful let's-get-this-settled fashion. "He is our—what do you call it? Our Google man."

As he listens, Ato Tekle's brows rise, then scrunch again, ridged with anticipated effort. I can feel the magnetic pull of my old house only a hundred yards away, offering closure on three decades of waiting. But it seems there is no option except to wait a bit longer.

"Were you here in the time of the revolution?" I ask Ato Tekle, who begins to nod before the Arsenal minister has translated. He opens his eyes wide and sucks in his breath in an affirmative "Awo." Then he launches into a lengthy explanation, speaking in Amharic rather than Gofa, so that Sahle and Temesgen can follow along.

Sahle and his son listen with rapt attention, lifting their heads to show they are catching what is being said. Luke stands patiently to the side, thinking I-am-still-hardly-out-of-America thoughts. I just look at Ato Tekle's earnest eyes, wishing I understood Amharic better.

The translation, when it comes back to us, is worth the wait. Ato Tekle was here right through the revolution, except for two or three years when he stayed in Addis, hoping to begin a career as a policeman. While he was being trained, he realized he would probably get drafted instead, forced to fight in the Eritrean war. Every young male was getting conscripted. Some were hiding in attics or dressing as girls. So he came back to Bulki on a bus and hid in the woods. He stayed in the forests for half a year or more. It was too dangerous to show himself because he had been at the police academy. They had all his information: where he was from, where his parents lived, what school he had attended. All he could do was to meet his father at night in the woods to get food.

Luke's eyes are wide, amazed to be hearing this kind of story first-hand. It's one thing to have a dad who talks in the abstract about such events, but to be right here? To see the very man who went through it?

"Did you know the missionaries who lived here?" I ask Ato Tekle. "Is there any chance you met my parents, Dr. Bascom and Kay? Could you have seen me or my brother—two high school boys? One with dark hair—that's me. And one with yellow hair?"

As the Arsenal minister translates, Ato Tekle looks from me to his colleague, frowning. He stares at me closely. He shakes his head. He says something else, and I think I hear a couple of names I recognize.

"Did he say Forsberg?" I blurt out, and Ato Tekle lifts his chin in a quick nod.

"My parents knew the Forsbergs, too. They were some of the first to come to Bulki back before even the Italians invaded. But how would Ato Tekle know them?"

The Arsenal minister smiles. "He says that his father still has cows that came from the cow of the Forsbergs. He says they are good for milk. Like American ice cream."

"Awo!" Ato Tekle adds, nodding eagerly. I can feel his delight—his relief really—at stumbling onto this common ground, something that we both know.

As we walk down the slope and across the small glade, Ato Tekle warms up, explaining through translation that he also knew the Stinsons, the missionaries who lived on the station just before us. And he tells a story I have never heard before. Apparently, the reason the Stinsons left, at least as Ato Tekle understands, is because of a single man that the mission sponsored at Bible school, a man who graduated and returned convinced that he should take charge. This man, after the fall of the emperor, told the Stinsons and other missionaries that they were no longer needed, that it was time to give over the leadership to locals, to him in particular. He was very forceful, and he convinced the other staff to quit their positions at the clinic and the mission school, going down to the large town in the valley, where they lodged formal complaints with the authorities. Then, paradoxically, the same mission-trained graduate started making a reputation for himself among the local communist cadre, gaining enough trust to become a regional commander. After he was confronted by old church friends, he put them in jail. He took two wives. And he began to denounce all Christians as enemies of the state, calling for their arrest. It was for this reason, Ato Tekle thinks, that the Stinsons and all the other missionaries left, maybe even my own parents.

I listen with surprise, having never heard this story about why Bulki was left unstaffed prior to our arrival. I consider sharing the version I was given back in 1977, but we have now arrived at the house itself, which demands all my attention. Standing next to the weary structure, I can't shake the odd impression that smoke is spilling from under the eaves, perhaps caused by wisps of low-lying cloud. The side porch, with torn screens, is strewn with thousands of eucalyptus acorns. Half the glass sheets are broken out of their multi-pane frames. And a tin awning sags sideways over the gaping front door so that we have to

duck to enter. Still, though, it is here, intact since my parents abandoned it.

I step inside and I realize my senses are not playing tricks on me;
I can actually smell smoke. I see it gathered against the ceiling. But
why? Is the building, after standing all these years, finally going to go
up in flames, burning as I feared it would when I was only three and
the farmers set fire to the mountain slopes, clearing old growth for a
new season of tilling?

I ask, "Where is the smoke coming from?" and Ato Tekle explains,
through translation, that a farmer is allowed to stay on the compound
to maintain it for the church since it is church property now, given
back by the government. He thinks the man and his wife live in the
stone-walled basement, using the cold upstairs as a storage shed.
Maybe the farmer's wife has a fire down below, he says, to stay warm
or to make pots. He has heard she sells pots.

Conscious of these mysterious residents, we all walk more lightly,
tiptoeing into the living room, where I can look out the broken picture window into the vast valley, remembering Julie Andrews on the
record player, singing ecstatically about the mountains being full of
music.

Next, we go down the short hall that leads into the bedroom
where Nat and I slept, and in the middle of that empty room is a long
wooden plow with an iron blade, stored there for the next season of
planting. The smoke is very thick here, and we cough. I want a photo,
though, of someone holding this wonderful old tool, brought right
into my former bedroom. Sahle's son, Temesgen, lifts the wooden
handle and acts as if he is a farmer in a field. I ask him to step back to
get the whole thing into the picture. He shuffles backward into straw.
I ask him to step back just one more foot, and suddenly there is a
strange clattering. A sheet of tin upends, and without a word, Temesgen falls straight down, dropping to his waist, where one leg catches,
splayed out across the floor.

Temesgen clings to the lowered handle of the plow, his eyes wide
with shock. Smoke billows around him as if threatening to burst into
flame. Then we grab him at the armpits and hoist him out of the unexpected hole.

Amazing. Underneath, in the old storage space, is a pit of live coals,
red-hot and sending up flickers of yellow. Like a glimpse into Dante's

inferno, it smolders away in this mysterious underworld, where the new occupants, still not visible, must be firing their pots as they step out on errands.

We all laugh as Temesgen rubs his bruised buttock, amused that he came so close to disaster. We return the tin to its place over the hole and step carefully back into the living room. Then I notice some Amharic script scrawled right onto the wall in charcoal. What do the words say, I ask. And Temesgen, still rubbing his sore rump, tells me that it seems to say: "How beautiful it was when the missionaries were here."

"Are you sure?" I ask.

"Yes, that's what it says!"

Ato Tekle, watching this conversation, suddenly interjects something apologetic. He appears pained as he looks toward me, launching into an explanation and stopping only briefly for translation. Eventually I get the full story. Not long ago, all the Christians of the area gathered here on the mountain, feeling bad about how the missionaries had been treated. Some felt guilty about what they had done to frighten away the missionaries. By the way, he explains, that man who went down the mountain and became a communist, he was here. He confessed after the fall of Mengistu. He came to church, crawling on his knees. Today, he has been accepted back.

I must look incredulous because Ato Tekle adds that he is a good man; he has changed.

But anyway, he continues, the church members of the area gathered here at the old mission station, and the ones who had remained silent through the revolution, afraid to take a stance, confessed. So did the ones who had condemned the missionaries. They prayed together, right here on the mountain, facing west toward Canada and the United States, and they asked God's forgiveness for what they had done. They asked which way was New Zealand and Australia, and they prayed for the missionaries down there, asking God to bless them. They asked which way was England, and they prayed in that direction.

Listening to him, I feel almost choked by emotion. Such graciousness. The same graciousness I had felt over thirty years ago when I walked down the mountain with my father to worship at the church in the savannah, missing the MAF plane. The same graciousness that

Joseph, the clinic dresser, showed when he helped my parents to pack and fly out of Bulki, never to return.

I say to Ato Tekle, "You know, my parents never felt that the church here was against them. They had great admiration for the believers. They felt welcomed and challenged in good ways. We could leave Ethiopia; you could not. And we were amazed to see how strong people were during such a hard time."

He listens with his characteristic concentration, as if working on a still-not-resolved equation. Then he nods in quiet comprehension.

I say to him, "I will tell my parents about the people praying for forgiveness, but I am sure they will want you to know that they feel the need for forgiveness, too. When they left Ethiopia, they felt like they were abandoning the church—their own brothers and sisters. I, too, could use your prayers. I am not always faithful. I have doubts that keep me from living how I want."

He nods with sober concern. "I will pray for you," he says. And he lifts his hands toward the heavens, saying, "God is always listening."

I have only one question left, which I have been putting off, although I want to ask it, especially of this man, who lived right through the worst of it all, right here, hiding in the forest. I turn to him now, primed to say what has been rattling around inside me like a rock in a hubcap: "After all those troubles under Mengistu—you know, the fighting and the persecution and the hiding—what do you think? Was there anything good about the revolution?"

The Arsenal minister translates and Ato Tekle's face gathers in concentration. I anticipate that he will shake his head emphatically. I wait for that response. But to my surprise, he nods slowly and thoughtfully.

"Yes," he finally says, and I hardly need a translation as he lifts both hands again in a God-be-praised fashion, facing toward the broken picture window before gesturing outward toward the vast open expanse of the valley, arms open.

"Now," he says, "we have our own land."

Bibliography

Achebe, Chinua. *Things Fall Apart*. New York: Anchor Books Edition, 1994. Print.

Bascom, Kay. *Hidden Triumph in Ethiopia*. Pasadena: William Carey Library, 2001. Print.

Coleman, Daniel. *The Scent of Eucalyptus*. Fredericton, NB: Goose Lane Editions, 2003. Print.

Cotterell, F. Peter. *Born at Midnight*. Chicago: Moody Press, 1973. Print.

Cumbers, John B. *Living with the Red Terror: Missionary Experiences in Communist Ethiopia*. Kearney, NE: Morris Publishing, 1996. Print.

Eshete, Tibebe. *The Evangelical Movement in Ethiopia: Resistance and Resilience*. Waco, TX: Baylor University Press, 2009. Print.

Forsberg, Malcolm. *Land Beyond the Nile*. New York: Harper and Brothers Publishers, 1958. Print.

————. *Last Days on the Nile*. Philadelphia: J. B. Lippincott Company, 1966. Print.

Giorgis, Dawit Wolde. *Red Tears: War, Famine, and Revolution in Ethiopia*. Trenton, NJ: Red Sea Press, 1988. Print.

Hailie, Rebecca. *Held at a Distance: My Rediscovery of Ethiopia*. Chicago: Academy Chicago Publishers, 2007. Print.

Hancock, Graham. *The Sign and the Seal: The Quest for the Lost Ark of the Covenant*. New York: Touchstone Books, 1993. Print.

Hochschild, Adam. *King Leopold's Ghost*. Boston: Houghton Mifflin Company, 1998. Print.

Kapuscinski, Ryszard. *The Emperor*. Reissued ed. New York: Vintage Books, 1989. Print.

Lambie, Thomas A., M.D. *A Doctor Without a Country*. New York: Fleming H. Revell, Company, 1939. Print.

Last, Geoffrey, and Richard Pankhurst. *A History of Ethiopia in Pictures*. Addis Ababa: Oxford University Press, 1969. Print.

Man, C. Griffith. *Art of Ethiopia*. London: Paul Holberton Publishers, 2006. Print.

McLellan, Dick. *Warriors of Ethiopia: Heroes of the Gospel in the Omo River Valley*. Kingsgrove, Australia: Kingsgrove Press, 2006. Print.

Mengiste, Maaza. *Beneath the Lion's Gaze*. New York: W. W. Norton Company, 2010. Print.

Meredith, Martin. *The State of Africa: A History of Fifty Years of Independence*. London: The Free Press, 2005. Print.

Mezlekia, Nega. *Notes from the Hyena's Belly*. New York: Picador, 2002. Print.

Moorehead, Alan. *The White Nile*. New York: Harper and Brothers Publishers, 1960. Print.

Pakenham, Thomas. *The Scramble for Africa: White Man's Conquest of the Dark Continent from 1876 to 1912*. New York: Avon Books, 1991. Print.

Verghese, Abraham. *Cutting for Stone*. New York: Alfred A. Knopf, 2009. Print.

sightline books
The Iowa Series in Literary Nonfiction